Published by:
AVID Publications
7 Garth Boulevard
Bebington
Wirral
Merseyside
L63 5LS
United Kingdom
Tel: 051-645 2047

GW00717075

Further copies of this book can be obtained from the above.

ISBN No. 0 9521020 2 1

Edited by William David Roberts

By the same Author... Life at Lairds   ISBN No.   0 9521020 1 3

Cover Photo - Launch of Polaris Submarine, *HMS REVENGE*, 1968. Author Photo by Bobby Shacklady.

*I dedicate this book to my late father,
John Ivor Roberts, a Cammell Lairds cranedriver
for most of his life; I believe he would have liked it.
Also for my son Luke, with all my love.*

THE AUTHOR

I was born in Birkenhead and lived in Tranmere, a stone's throw from Cammell Lairds Green Lane gate, until my early twenties. My father, Ivor Roberts, was a cranedriver on the new 100 ton slipway cranes that the company commissioned in the mid sixties.

I served my apprenticeship as a Fitter with the company in the late 1960's, early 1970's. I left the company soon after this but have always maintained a keen interest in the fortunes of the company; I always say that I have a soft spot for Cammell Lairds.

Apart from maritime history, my other interests are squash, computing and the poetry of Byron. Now married with a family, I still live on the Wirral, working as a teacher.

Foreword

The Cammell Laird shipyard has always been the heart and soul of Birkenhead's manufacturing industry. As David roberts points out in this stimulating book, there are not many families in the area where lives have not been touched at some point by the yard. This book traces the history of the yard through the Polaris years and raises the question of whether the concentration on Polaris may have, in the long term, hindered the yard as much as it helped it.

A quarter of a century further on the problems facing the yard today seem familiar to the reader of David Roberts's book. As defence industries in the country face an uncertain future with the end of the cold war and the scaling down of defence commitments implicit in the so-called "peace dividend", it is important that Lairds diversify into other areas.

Cammell Laird indeed has a history of great innovation. The Laird family were pioneers in maritime technology. The *Robert F. Stockton*, built at Lairds, was the first ship to be fitted with Ericsson's patented propeller device. This small vessel became the first screw steamer to cross the Atlantic. Lairds also built the first iron ship owned by HM Government, *HMS Dover* in 1840. Lairds also completed the world's first ever all-welded deep sea vessel, the *Fullagar* of 1920. In 1960 Cammell Laird manufactured the first guided missile destroyer to be powered by gas turbines. It is with this record of innovation and adaptation that Lairds now looks for a new owner and the start of another chapter in its long and distinguished career.

Frank Field
House of Commons
May 1992

Acknowledgements

So many people and organisations have helped me with this work that it is difficult to be concise in my thanks, but particular acknowledgements are due to...

Cammell Laird Shipbuilders
...for giving me access to their archive material and the loan of numerous photographs.

Mr. Frank Lindstrom
...of the ship design office at Cammell Lairds, part time archivist for the company, without whose knowledge and assistance this book would not have been possible.

Robert White Johnson
...retired former Chairman and Managing Director of the company for the use of his personal papers and photographs and for his memories.

D.L.P. (Dai) Evans
...a former Commander of Polaris submarines, for using his specialised knowledge and editing the text.

My wife Denise
...for taking second place to Cammell Lairds and allowing me the time.

Mark Rickards
...my very good friend. For talking and being there.

Mr. John Lea (Fotovideo)
...for his photographic expertise, encouragement and his sense of humour.

Andy Haughey
...for his computer expertise and his advice.

...and my special gratitude to the people of Birkenhead and the men who built Polaris submarines.

"There is no firm (on the Mersey) that has attained greater eminance than the Messers. Laird, of Birkenhead. The distinguished services rendered by that firm to the science of naval architecture have been recognised over and over again not only by our Government, but by many foreign potentates. It is only proper, therefore, that the Messers. Lairds should here be acknowledged as the pioneers of the iron ship-building trade of the Mersey, and, in placing something like a connected history of their career, and of the achievements which have made their names "familiar in our mouths as household words" we shall be undertaking the performance of a hitherto unattempted task ."

Extract from a decription of The Birkenhead Iron Works.
from "Practical Magazine" June 1874.

CONTENTS

A Chronology

1824 Founding of Birkenhead Iron Works by William Laird at Wallasey Pool.

1828 John Laird joins the firm. Now Wm. Laird & Son. First iron ship built...the WYE. A 90 foot lighter for the Irish Inland Steam Navigation Co.

1832 First ocean going voyage by an iron vessel, the *ALBURKAH*, taken by Macgregor Laird on his first West African Expedition.

1837 First screw driven ship the ROBERT F. STOCKTON.

1840 First iron ship to be owned by British Government, the *DOVER*.

1846 Building of the famous paddle man-of-war *BIRKENHEAD* for the British Government.

1852 Macgregor Laird founds African Steamship Co. Lairds build 5 steamers for this company. Forerunner, Faith, Hope, Charity and Northern Light. This company was later to become the world famous Elder Dempster Company.

1856 Lloyds of London issue first specification for iron ships.

1858 Wallasey land required for development of docks and taken over by the newly formed Mersey Docks and Harbour Board. John Laird is appointed to M. D. H. B. as it's government nominee. Lairds move to new site between Monks Ferry and Tranmere Pool.

1861 John Laird retires from the business. Control goes to sons William, John and Henry.

1862 Launch of the *ALABAMA* the infamous raider for the Confederates in the American civil war. Vessel no. 290, launched as the *ENRICA*. Paradoxically, a wooden ship.

1863 John Laird becomes first M.P. for Birkenhead. Company now known as Laird Brothers.

1874 Death of John Laird.

1900 Becomes a public company Laird Brothers and Company Ltd.

1903 Amalgamation with Charles Cammell, a Sheffield based Steel manufacturer. Now Cammell Laird and Co. Ltd.

1910 End of Laird family connection. Last "Laird" Chairman, J. Macgregor Laird dies. New head of company is William Lionel Hitchens.

1915 Lairds build first experimental submarine the *E41*.

1917 King George V and Queen Mary visit the yard to celebrate output of over 150,000 tons of war shipping.

1920 Completion of first ever all welded vessel the Fullagar, for the Anchor and Brocklebank Line.

1922 New Managing Director Mr. Robert (later Sir Robert) Stewart Johnson, father of Robert White Johnson the Managing Director of Lairds during "the polaris years."

1927 Completion of Her Majesty's Battleship Rodney, launched by H.R.H. Princess Mary.

1931 Depression sees only one vessel under construction at Lairds. Workforce approx. 2000.

1934 Lairds builds it's 1000th ship for the Booth Steamship Co. of Liverpool; A 5000 ton cargo liner *CLEMENT*.

1935 Order for the first ship to be designed and built as an aircraft carrier, Ark Royal. Launched 2 years later and watched by an estimated crowd of 30,000 people.

1939 Launch of the Mauretania for the Cunard Company.

1939 Loss of 99 lives when Lairds built submarine Thetis fails to surface on sea trials off Anglesey. The worst submarine disaster in British History.

1940 Robert Stewart Johnson becomes Chairman.

1939-1945 Lairds build 106 fighting ships. An average of one every 20 days.

1951 Robert Stewart Johnson dies. His son Robert White Johnson becomes Managing Director of the company. J. C. Mather becomes chairman.

1954 Company now becomes Cammell Laird and Co. (Shipbuilders and Engineers.)

1955 Completion of Lairds second Ark Royal aircraft carrier.

1959 Launch of the Windsor Castle by H.M. Queen Mother, for the Union Castle Company.

1960 Launch of first ever gas-turbine powered guided missile destroyer Devonshire for the Admiralty.

1962 Princess Alexandra opens new Princess Dock. Then the largest privately owned dry dock in Britain. Amalgamation with local firm of Grayson, Rollo and Clover, ship repairers and engineers.

1963 Award of contract, from H. M. Government to build two nuclear powered Polaris Submarines.

1964 Keel laid of ship no. 1316. Polaris submarine Renown.

1965 Formation of Cammell Laird Group with subsidiaries... Cammell Laird and Co. (Ship-builders and Engineers) and Cammell Laird (Ship repairers). Keel laid of ship no. 1317, Polaris submarine Revenge.

1967 Workforce numbers almost 12,000. Keel laid of ship no. 1330. Hunter Killer nuclear submarine (non-polaris) Conqueror. Later to gain enormous publicity as the vessel that sank the Argentine battleship the General Belgrano in the South Atlantic during the Falklands conflict.

1968 Handover of H.M.S Renown.

1969 Handover of H.M.S. Revenge.

1970 Financial reconstruction of the company. H.M. Government take 50% interest in Cammell Laird & Co. (Shipbuilders and Engineers). The shipbuilding company ceases to be a part of the Laird Group.

1972 Company now Cammell Laird Shipbuilders Ltd. Old camel logo replaced with CL monogram design. Government announces plans to financially assist Lairds modernisation programme.

1976 Completion of HMS Birmingham first of 3 type 42 destroyers for Royal Navy.

1977 Company nationalised as part of British Shipbuilders.

1978 Completion of modernisation programme. New covered 145m x 107m x 50m high "construction hall".

1985 Company denationalised to becomes a subsidiary of Vickers Shipbuilding and Engineering Ltd. (V.S.E.L.)

1991/2 The company workforce numbers under 2,000. Three conventional submarines of the Upholder class are under construction. The first, *HMS UNSEEN* was handed over in 1991. *HMS URSULA*, second of the trio, was handed over in May 1992.

1993 The last submarine to be built at Cammell Lairds, *HMS UNICORN*, was handed over to the Navy in July. At the end of July 1993, Cammell Lairds Shipyard closed down.

From the beginning...

In 1963, Cammell Laird at Birkenhead, the only large shipbuilding yard on Merseyside, received a major government contract to build two of the five Polaris submarines commissioned by the Macmillan government in pursuit of an independent nuclear deterrent. According to Macmillan, these vessels would "provide a weapon that would last for a generation".

Only now, more than a quarter of a century later, is Britain building Trident submarines to replace Polaris, indicating that, in terms of longevity, Macmillan was right. The historical and political reasons for Britain's independent nuclear policy are however, peripheral to this book. Its prime focus is the Cammell Laird company and its workforce during these "Polaris years".

Britain was to have built 5 Polaris submarines and of the four contenders to build these vessels; Scotts at Greenock, the Naval Dockyard at Chatham, Vickers Armstrong at Barrow and Cammell Laird at Birkenhead only the latter pair were successful in obtaining the contracts to build 2 vessels a piece. The order for the fifth was held in abeyance and subsequently cancelled in March 1965 as part of the new Labour governments defence expenditure review.

Vickers was to be the lead yard. A lead yard is considered to possess sufficient experience and ability to be the senior partner of a shipbuilding contract that is allotted to more than one shipyard. Vickers did possess the required experience of building nuclear powered, though non-polaris submarines; they had already completed *HMS DREADNOUGHT* and were in the process of building *HMS VALIANT*.

Two weeks after the announcement in May 1963, Mr. Robert White Johnson, the Chairman of Cammell Laird, announced at the launching of a conventional diesel powered submarine *HMS OPPOSSUM*, that the nuclear contract promised "something in the region of 3,000 jobs", in addition the four vessels were likely to cost "in the region of £200 million."(1)

5

The Birkenhead shipbuilders numbers for these vessels, to be named *RENOWN* and *REVENGE* were 1316 and 1317 respectively and an indication of the importance of this contract to Lairds is given by the time taken from contract order to the handover of *HMS REVENGE*, a period of six and a half years.

During this time the company built a number of cross-channel car ferries, one bulk carrier and a few small cargo vessels. Certainly no other major contracts were to pass through Lairds during this time and detailed reference is made to this fact later in the book.

The contract was to be "the greatest challenge in the history of the company".(2) The company was going to have to make changes as such vessels had never before been constructed outside of the United States. Both shipbuilders embarked on a task which involved an expansion of facilities, an increase in staff, a change in the structure and a profound effect upon the standards of work and the nature of management operations. This book is concerned with those changes in Lairds. It deals with how the company and its workforce coped with them at the time, and what bearing they would have had, if any, on the future of the Birkenhead yard. It is an attempt to look both at and behind the good times that were apparent in the yard, whilst holding onto the knowledge that, with hindsight, the end of the Polaris contract might have been the beginning of the end for Cammell Laird as a major shipbuilding company nationally and locally.

A detailed examination of the workforce will show that they were well aware of the temporal nature of the job and so tried to make the most of a good thing while it lasted.

That history often repeats itself is well known. Thus a reasonable way of looking at latter day Lairds is to first attempt to understand the story of the company from the very beginning. The hallmark of its history is one of perseverance against the odds, sticking to its beliefs and of being unafraid to try something new.

The word *FIRST* occurs so many times when looking at the yards history that is hard to believe that no lasting record of the achievements of this company has been undertaken before. The company itself did produce it's *BUILDERS OF GREAT SHIPS* book in 1959, and in the mid 1970's, whilst nationalised and a member of British Shipbuilders, a commemorative brochure of the first 150 years of the yard. Sadly these two company publications are becoming increasingly rare and so, in part this book is an attempt to rectify matters before examining in detail part of the modern era in Lairds.

Pioneering determination is really the only way to describe the story of Lairds shipyard. This spirit is evident throughout its history right up to the 1960's, when Polaris was the yards last great pioneering exploit. The fundamental evolution of seagoing vessels runs exactly in line with Lairds efforts, from wood to iron, sail to steam, rivets to welding and from paddle to screw. Lairds were first, or at the forefront of trying to ring the changes. It was no mean feat when faced by diehards and doubting Thomases, "to keep your head when all about you are losing theirs," as Kipling would have put it.

As the Laird family were building their maritime "firsts" using new methods and technology, they were also building the town of Birkenhead. The town as characterised by wide roads leading to the town and coming together in the magnificence of Hamilton Square. Gas lighting was much in evidence and every dwelling had running water.

Laird brought more than industry to the industrial revolution, he brought health and care into the reality of town living. To Laird it made sense to have a contented and reliable workforce at a time when men of vision were the exception; in many parts of the country industrial workers were less fortunate.

The yard began life in 1824 as the Birkenhead Iron works. Its founder was William Laird, a Scot, who guided the Birkenhead Iron Works towards building their first ship in 1828, the iron vessel *WYE* for the Irish Inland Steam Navigation Company. Even then Laird was not afraid of trying something new, and for the remainder of the 19th Century persisted in building iron ships and steamers in the face of doubting shipowners and a trepidatious Admiralty.

Lairds clients grew. The General Steam Navigation Company

took possession of the RAINBOW in 1837, which, at 600 tons was the largest iron ship ever. Whilst under construction the *RAINBOW* was used by the then Astronomer Royal, Professor Airey, in the early stages of experimenting with reliable compasses. Laird realised that iron ships would not get the proper recognition that they deserved, unless the problems of compass deviation could be resolved.

In 1838 Lairds completed the *ROBERT. F. STOCKTON*, the first ship to be fitted with a patented propeller device invented by the Swedish engineer John Ericcson. This tiny vessel, a 33 ton river boat, established another Laird first, becoming the earliest screw steamer to cross the Atlantic.

To be accurate the majority of the voyage was made without using the screw propeller. At this stage engines were still regarded as an adjunct to sail which remained the main method of propulsion.

Lairds had built a total of 17 ships by now, but it was hard going - ship owners and insurers still viewed the iron ship with some distrust.

In 1840 lairds built *HMS DOVER*, the first iron ship owned by Her Majesty's government. Six years later saw the completion of the famous man-of-war *BIRKENHEAD*. At 1400 tons the *BIRKENHEAD* was eventually converted into a troop carrier because the weight of her guns was considered too heavy for an already heavy ship.

She was later wrecked on a reef in Simons Bay, off the coast of South Africa. The display of heroism as the troops fell into seried ranks to allow the women and children off the stricken vessel is forever captured in Thomas Hemys painting "The sinking of the Birkenhead" , a second copy of which, painted by Hemys, now hangs in the Williamson Art Gallery in the town.

A river paddle steamer was built for the famous explorer David Livingstone, who actually visited the yard. To monitor the progress of the vessel. She was named the *MA ROBERT*, the Africans name for Mrs. Livingstone and was used for the great mans expedition up the Zambezi in 1858.

The Laird family themselves were to leave their mark locally, nationally and internationally. Locally in the town of Birkenhead, streets, squares and schools bear the Laird name or an ancestral Laird nomenclature. John Laird, William's son, became the first M.P. for Birkenhead in 1863 and was re-elected in the next three general elections.

In 1862 John Laird perhaps forsook any potential he may have had for a knighthood by undertaking the infamous contract to build the raidership *ALABAMA* for the Confederates in the American Civil war, despite protests from the American Ambassador to Britain. Surprisingly, a wooden ship, she was to wreak havoc among Union shipping in the next 2 years before being sunk off Cherbourg in 1864. Today the Alabama is the subject of much debate by interested salvage parties on both sides of the Atlantic, but the prospects of raising her is felt by some to be tantamount to condoning slavery, one of the mainstays of confederate philosophy.

Whatever the outcome of these plans, the culpability of Lairds in the breaching of Britain's neutrality during the American Civil war was highlighted when, in 1871, and after a 5 year legal wrangle, the British Government were forced to pay compensation to the by then "UNITED" States for the damage done by the *ALABAMA* (and her sisters, the non Lairds built *FLORIDA* and *SHANANDOAH*). The sum involved was 15.5 million dollars which was paid in gold, a staggering sum even then.

Perhaps the most renowned of all the Laird family for his exploits overseas was John's brother, Macgregor. In 1832 he undertook an exploratory trip to West Africa in the *ALBURKAH*, an iron vessel of just 70 feet by 13 feet with a draft of 6 feet and fitted with a 16 H.P. engine.

ALBURKAH was accompanied by another ship, the *QUORRA* and by a sailing vessel the *COLUMBINE*. The expedition returned to Liverpool having lost 39 of the 48 men who started out through fever and dysentery. The *ALBURKAH* acquitted herself well thus further demonstrating the value of iron ships.

Macgregor Laird founded the African Steamship Company in 1852, an antecedent of the great shipping empire of Elder Dempster. Lairds built 5 steamers for this company, the *FORERUNNNER, FAITH, HOPE, CHARITY* and *NORTHERN LIGHT*.

John Laird died in 1874. On the day of his funeral work in the town stopped, shops closed for business and almost half of the 3000 men employed at the yard fell in behind the funeral carriages. The streets were packed with sad onlookers paying their respects. A publicly subscribed statue was erected in his memory opposite Birkenhead Town Hall, in Hamilton Square, itself named after an ancestor on his mothers side who was once Archbishop of Scotland.

The shipbuilding business remained in the control of the Laird family until 1903. Admiralty rational then was for "package deal" orders; in other words to order a complete ship from one manufacturer rather than place orders with a number of diffuse specialist suppliers. One such specialist supplier was the Sheffield based steel manufacturer Charles Cammell, rapidly making his name in the third quarter if the 19th Century as an important supplier of armour plating.
One of Cammell's biggest customers was Laird Brothers as it was then known, and so it made sense to present a united consortium to the Admiralty.

A new company was formed, Cammell Laird and Company Limited, which, after some difficult early years, went from strength to strength servicing both naval and merchant ship orders. The Admiralty ordered the 23,090 ton battleship *AUDACIOUS*, later to be sunk in WW1, and in 1912 the largest floating dock in the world with a lifting capability of 32,000 tons.

Interestingly, one of the first experimental submarines, the *E41*, was Laird built in 1915. Merchant ship work was just as important with orders from Peninsular and Orient for the cargo liners *KHIVA* and *KHYBER*, and the Isle of Man Steam Packet Co., for ferries such as the *KING ORRY* launched in 1913. The shipyards first train ferry the *LEONARD* was launched soon after for the Canada Trans-Continental Railway Company.

1908 saw the end of the Laird family connection, the last family chairman of the company, J. Macgregor Laird, died in 1910.

The various disarmament conferences between the wars generally saw a fall in Admiralty work but with some notable exceptions. In 1927 *HMS RODNEY* was completed and six years later so was *HMS ACHILLES*. The latter was renowned for her part in running down the German Pocket Battleship the *GRAF SPEE* during world war two.

Commercial contracts helped the yard survive the depression until the middle thirties. The 17,750 ton passenger liner *DE GRASS* was built for the French company La Companie Generale Transatlantique during these lean times.

Of all Lairds pioneering efforts perhaps the greatest technological achievement was the completion of the first ever all welded deep sea vessel in the world the *FULLAGAR*. She was made for the Anchor and Brocklebank line in 1920. In the same year Cammell Laird patented a special protective mask for use by welders.

The middle 30's brought the orders for some of Lairds most famous ships, the first purpose built aircraft carrier *ARK ROYAL*, was completed in 1938 and the largest ship ever built in England at that time, the 34,000 ton *MAURETANIA* was completed for the Cunard Company, in 1939.

As in any catalogue of achievement there are occasional lows to be recorded and perhaps the most tragic event in all of the yards history was the loss of the submarine *THETIS* on sea trials off Anglesey in 1939. The worst submarine disaster in British History. The 99 lives lost included numerous Lairdsmen taking part in the trials.

The second world war brought orders thick and fast to Lairds and in all the company built 106 fighting ships, including the *PRINCE OF WALES*, aboard which Winston Churchill and President Roosevelt signed the Atlantic Charter. The special affection that was felt for the *PRINCE OF WALES* is shown by the reaction of her sponsor H.R.H. the Princess Royal, Mary, on hearing the news of this ships loss from a Japanese torpedo. In a letter to R. S. Johnson from Harewood House Leeds, she wrote..

".....the tragic news of the sinking of this super ship, with the loss of life of so many gallant officers and men. I do so feel for you very deeply and for Messrs.. Cammell Laird and all those who built this ship..."

The company of Cammell Laird actually received commendations from The Admiralty for it's wartime work, specifically for it's repair work on the Battleship *BARHAM* and the aircraft carrier *ILLUSTRIOUS*.

Between the end of the second world war and the 1960's the company's fortunes were largely dependent upon merchant work as shipowners replaced their war casualties and vessels they had been unable to pension off due to the wartime priority for naval building.

Lairds were building for Shaw Savill and Albion Company the *CORINTHIC*, *CERAMIC*, and *CARNATIC*, for the Blue Star Line the quartet of *STAR* boats, the *ARGENTINA*, *BRAZIL*, *URUGUAY* and *PARAGUAY STARS*, and many oil tankers for various clients.

Some naval work was received, perhaps the most significant of which was the second *ARK ROYAL* aircraft carrier completed in 1955. Almost 50,000 people attended the launching ceremony of this ship, performed, for the first time in the yards history, by a Queen of England, Queen Elizabeth I, now the Queen Mother.

The last great passenger liner to be built at Birkenhead was launched by the same sponsor in 1959. The *WINDSOR CASTLE* for the Union Castle Company was an example of the elegance of Lairds design and the skills of the workforce.

In 1960 Cammell Laird produced yet another first for the Royal Navy. The guided missile destroyer *DEVONSHIRE*, powered by Gas Turbines, was the first warship to use this form of propulsion. Two years later the massive Princess dry dock, then the largest privately owned dry dock in Britain, was officially opened by the Princess Alexandra.

By 1965 Cammell Laird was the largest company in the Cammell Laird Group. It is right at the end of this period 1969 / 70, as the Polaris submarines were sailing away, that the foundation of the yard and the name of Laird were to be badly shaken. The Polaris years were undoubtedly good ones, but when these vessels were completed Lairds faced a liquidity crisis so severe, that Her Majesty's government had to bale out the company and acquire 50% of the equity in the shipbuilding arm of the Laird Group, that is Cammell Laird and Co. Shipbuilders and Engineers. This company was then severed from the Laird Group to spend the next 15 years in the wilderness of nationalisation and denationalisation before becoming part of the Vickers Shipbuilding and Engineering Ltd. Consortium in the mid 1980's; in effect a subsidiary company of their 'elder brother' lead yard of twenty years earlier, following, perhaps ironically, a similar rationale to that which brought Laird and Cammell together in 1903.

Certainly the period was a dynamic one, but a second and central issue is the role of the workforce itself and their attitudes. It is essential to look at this period specifically and at the men who worked on the Polaris project. In particular to try to reflect their attitudes to their work, their management and to the Polaris organisation.

The 1960's may be considered too recent a period to make an objective assessment. The Mersey was very much in the mind of the nation through the emergence of the Beatles and other Merseyside groups. When Denis Healey, Minister for Defence in 1963 attended the launch of 1316 (*RENOWN*) he recognised this fact in his speech..."it is good to see that one side of the Mersey has produced a yellow submarine whilst the other has built Polaris.."(3)

The problems with compiling a book of this nature are the immediacy of events, the absence of material and the sensitivity that many still have towards the "Polaris years". I have had to rely a great deal on interviews. Despite innumerable specialists, new techniques such as critical path analysis, milestone incentives and hitherto unprecedented quality control procedures the workforce building these submarines used as much art as they did science. Though building highly sophisticated fighting machines at the very cutting edge of technology, they also ensured for themselves high remuneration, often for little production.

These submarines were built on a cost-plus basis wherein the shipbuilder is not tied to a fixed price, as in the case of a commercial merchant vessel contract, but is paid for the actual costs incurred plus profit. This had an adverse effect on management who could so easily abrogate their authority and responsibility. This type of contract compounded the difficulties of an already complicated task, that of providing the country with an independent nuclear deterrent on time. One could easily mistake the whole management structure as being somewhat Heath Robinson and completely disorganised.

If it was so disorganised it begs the question whether this was a deliberate demonstration of resistance on the part of the workforce to get something for nothing? Or, given better leadership, would they have been much more efficient.

Whilst there appeared to be an enormous undercurrent running through the workforce to be paid whilst doing nothing, whilst either at home or in the local pub, there were also management problems born of this same 'easy money' mentality. A note of caution is necessary here, for as one interviewee told me...

"If the men were over the wall all the time then who was building the boats ?"(4)

The shipyard expression 'over the wall' refers to men that had clocked in at the yard, and were therefore being paid, but had left the premises without clocking off.

If this was true then it is an aspect of the Polaris years which warrants further investigation. Who was building the boats? Who was over the wall? Who wasn't? And who allowed all this to happen?

The period was a kind of Indian Summer for Cammell Lairds, incomparable with anything that had ever gone before in its long tradition as a shipyard, or with anything that happened subsequently. This was a time when money and overtime were easy to come by without over exertion. The Polaris boats were "like a great big juicy plum".(5) It seemed that neither management or the workforce questioned the situation; they were prepared to simply to gorge themselves during a period of opulence and free lunches.

The crucial aspect of these years revolves around the use and abuse of the cost-plus system. The painful economic problems experienced by Cammell Laird at the end of the Polaris contract occurred as a direct result of the company being locked into, and their blinkered approach to, a very lucrative and strategically important contract when, elsewhere, their competitors were assimilating new engineering methods and techniques in the building of ships.

The profits made from this contract were channelled away from the shipbuilding section of the group, perhaps a sound economic decision by the controlling board to save what they could and the devil take the hindmost. In hindsight this money should arguably have been re-invested in the shipyard enabling it to develop the capability to compete in world markets.

It is an interesting hypothesis.

But what is more certain in hindsight is that is that cost-plus contracts divorce a business from minding its business, sometimes with fatal results. Profitability is separated from production and people are separated from reality. Organisation and efficiency are the first to suffer and the only calculated company strategy is to ensure that the invoicing procedures include the required plus profit factor.

To write this book it was essential to establish as accurately as possible the feeling of the workforce and management in order to assess the yard itself, its work processes, and the controls that were exercised. The yard had its own identity, its own community spirit and its own class consciousness. It also possessed its own unique political awareness and conscience.

Numerous people from diverse sections of the workforce and management were interviewed to establish their views and it is these invaluable contributions that form the basis of the opinions expressed in the book. All of these men gave their permission to be recorded and without them this book would not have been possible. Brief outlines of these respondents are shown at the end of the book.

One phrase which came up with remarkable regularity in these interviews, and within almost any conversation with local people about the Polaris boats was the "Gravy Boats". They were regarded almost universally by both management and the workforce as the great providers of both work and income. The "Gravy Boats" are remembered as both objects of affection and derision, providing much that was good and bad. What was particularly useful to me was that they were remembered so clearly.

Through a mixture of personal interviews, Lairds archive material, published company accounts, local and national press reports and the work of others, I have sought to give an accurate account of the unique history of this famous yard. I am fortunate in having served a five year apprenticeship at Lairds between 1965 and 1970. For 2 of these years I was engaged on Polaris work. My father too was a shipyard worker and our home was located just 5 minutes walking time from the main gate at the bottom of Green Lane Birkenhead, close enough to almost fall out of bed and into work.

My formative years at Lairds were a very happy period in my life. I have very clear memories of those times as does any young man of his first work experience. In researching and writing this book I have tried to be objective and to avoid any particular bias in favour of management or the workforce. Above all I have tried to be faithful to the many people who took the time to give me their personal, and sometimes private, views.

Laird Brothers Yard in the 19th Century.

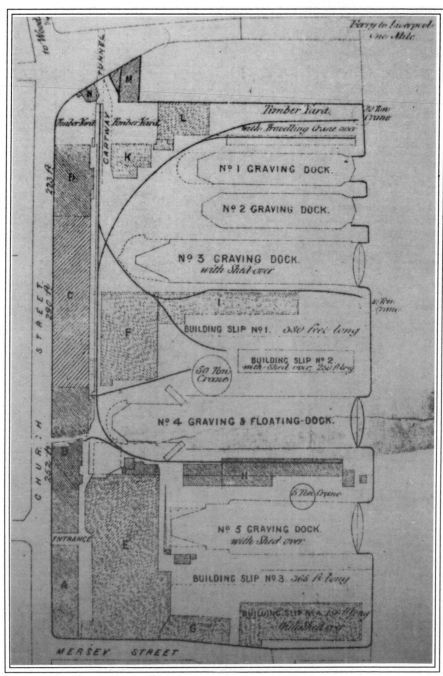

A plan of the shipyard in the mid 19th Century.

The paddle steamer *RAINBOW*, 1837, used in the early experiments to correct compass deviation on iron ships.

The Confederate Raidership *ALABAMA*, launched in 1862, much against the wishes of the American Government.

MA ROBERT was the name given to the paddle steamer built for the explorer David Livingstone. This was the African Natives name for Mrs. Livingstone.

John Lairds house on the corner of Hamilton Square, Birkenhead.

The Green Lane gate entrance to Lairds Yard covered with a temporary facade for the visit of King George V and Queen Mary in 1917 to celebrate the yards output of more than 150, 000 tons of war shipping. The Royal Crest under *BRITTANNIA* can just about be read.

Charles Cammell, a Sheffield based steel manufacturer and an important supplier to Lairds. The Cammell in Cammell Lairds arrived in 1903.

What the Polaris contract meant to the company.

"Lairds without a warship is like a church without a steeple" (6)

Having examined in the last chapter the early years of Cammell Laird it would be worth bearing in mind that the yard built its first iron ship in 1828 and with the approach of the Polaris years the yard therefore already had a long tradition of merchant and naval shipbuilding, including submarines. Equally in common with most other shipyards in Britain it has a very chequered industrial relations history.

Since 1959 the order book had been heavily biased towards merchant work, although some warships had been built too. The guided missile destroyer *DEVONSHIRE*, ship no. 1274 was handed over in 1962 and the frigate *AJAX* (1285) twelve months later. Three Oberon Class submarines had been completed by mid 1963 and Lairds built a multiplicity of vessels from Cable and Wireless boats to Mersey Ferries.(7) 1964 saw the beginning of the large tanker business at the yard come to an early end as the largest ship ever built at Birkenhead, the 71,950 ton *BRITISH ENSIGN* was handed over to B.P.

In the 1950's Cammell Laird Group shareholders enjoyed regular 14 and 15 percent dividends. And after a poor year in 1959 with only a 7% dividend the early 60's provided 10 to 12% dividends but on increased capital employed.(8)

It seems that in 1963, the company's centenary year since incorporation and the year the Polaris order was gained, the shipbuilders contribution to group profits was, to say the least, meagre.

At that time Michael M. Denny, the chairman of the group noted that the group "faced cut throat competition in the merchant field. Fortunately stockholders interests are fortified by the parent company having considerable financial investment in activities other than ship-building."(9)

Clearly 1963 was not a good year for the shipbuilding arm of the company. The yards contribution to group profits of £1.6 million was

23% of that sum, which seems reasonable until the shape of the 1963 trading account is presented in full.(10) Cammell Lairds return on turnover was a poor 3.1%. Under such circumstances there can be little doubt that the Polaris order seemed like manna from heaven.

fig.1	**Trading Results for Cammell Laird Group 1965**		
	Turnover £	Trading Results£	Return on Turnover
Cammell Laird & Co. Ltd	-	463, 354	-
Cammell Laird & Co. Ltd (S&E)	11, 907, 334	374, 143	3.1%
G. Rollo & Clover Ltd	1, 879, 528	34, 876	1.8%
The Patent Steel & Shaft Works Ltd	9, 944, 437	756, 286	7.6%
North Western Line (Mersey Ltd)	(5000)	(5000)	

fig.2	**Events Timetable**		
	Keel laid	Launch	Handover
1316 - *Renown*	June 1964	Feb 1967	Nov 1968
1317 - *Revenge*	May 1965	Mar 1968	Dec 1969

If 1963 was a poor year then, by comparison 1964 was disastrous. Cammell Laird and Co. (S+E) lost £726,303.(11)

It was only the advent of the Polaris contract which was to stop this decline.

Work began in earnest in June 1964. The programmed main events are as indicated in Table 2.

The keel of *RENOWN*, ship no 1316, was laid in June 1964 but the remaining six months of that year saw very little progress for two key reasons.

Firstly, during the remaining months of that year the weather was atrocious and the yard did not possess any covered facility to allow work to continue when such conditions prevailed. *RENOWN* was not launched until February 1967, 33 months after the keel was laid. Arguably this indicates that the work was too slow and that the 1964 winter construction period did not produce significant progress.

Covered facilities were available during the winters of 1965 and 1966 which would have sheltered the whole of the pressure hull. However a comparison with the progress made by Vickers building

RESOLUTION shows only one months difference.

Secondly, 1964 saw the only serious strike to occur during the Polaris years. This lasted for 3 months, from 16th March to 10th June and involved the shipwrights who wanted a comparability agreement so that they could be paid an additional shilling (5p) per hour to bring them in line with other trades within the yard. This strike would undoubtedly have delayed Laird's ability to prefabricate some sections of the Polaris hull and could also have delayed the laying of *RENOWN*'s keel. Without shipwrights a keel laying could not take place. The shipwrights returned to work without succeeding in their claim and *RENOWN*'s keel was laid a fortnight later.

From the evidence available, this was the last time up until the end of the Polaris years, that organised labour would capitulate on any matter.

These 2 factors would have affected Lairds ability to maintain any invoicing continuity for part payment. To be able to invoice the MOD was essential; laying the keel of the first boat was a significant milestone on which to do so.

fig.3 A Comparison of SSBN* Shipbuilder's Work (months)				
SSBN/Hull No.**	Builder	To launch	To completion	Total
Resolution (01)	Vickers	32	13	45
Renown (02)	Cammell Laird	33	22	55
Resolution (03)	Vickers	33	10	43
Renown (04)	Cammell Laird	35	21	56

*   SSBN is the designator for a Nuclear Powered Ballistic Missile Submarine
**   The Hull No is a Ministry of Defence designated number whilst the ship No is that used within a building yard.

Source: G. M. Dillon, *Dependence and Deterrence*, p 97. Gower 1983.

It is hard to understand Lairds management policy in 1964. The impending general election, which even to informed commentators looked like being a close run contest, must have been a very nervous time for Lairds. The key question was if Labour won, would they cancel the Polaris programme? Harold Wilson had stated on television that "if the programme has gone so far that the submarines could not be converted for other purposes, a Labour government would have to decide whether they should be completed as a contribution to NATO." (12) However despite this statement the local press were convinced that a Labour government would scrap the programme.

Birkenhead was a worried town. An editorial comment stated that ..."the Polaris projects are not ones about which Cammell Lairds can give public information, but it may be estimated that they would not be far advanced."(13) Such press comments, coinciding with a lengthy strike in the run up to a General Election produced a myriad possible strategy permutations.

Did Lairds engineer the strike so that in the event of a cancellation they would not be too deeply entrenched? Did the shipwrights union withdraw their labour at this time knowing the urgency of the building programme and the delicate political status of the programme? If the Polaris project was to be scrapped they might not have any leverage in the foreseeable future.

That year, 1964, it seemed that all concerned, both inside and outside Lairds, were playing a waiting game. According to one writer on the subject G. M. Dillon.(14) ... "nobody on the contractors side was enthusiastic about building up particular sorts of facilities and labour force levels with which they would have been saddled had a new government cancelled the programme or seriously reduced its size and scope." Another view, by John Simpson (15) goes further, stating that there was "a six month virtual suspension of construction work in 1964/ 5, when a political decision on the future of the British Polaris project was pending."

Lairds poor results in 1964 were publicly blamed on the strike and on..."the doubt engendered in the public mind about the Polaris programme not assisting specialist recruitment." (16)

This requirement for specialist recruitment may provide a further key to the fortunes of Cammell Laird and its workers at the time.

Polaris would change things, including men, techniques and attitudes - "shipbuilding is literally a dirty business and the general standards of cleanliness and precision were at odds with the more precise requirements of nuclear engineering....the contractual obligations which shipbuilders were required to assume gave the first public indication that the novelty of the Polaris task would materially affect standard practices."(17)

Don Siddorn, a millwright who had started work in Lairds in 1942 aged 15, said that......

"now I think back a little, all the things that went down at the yard could be drawn back to Polaris. It changed the whole system of the yard."(18)

What were these changes that the new orders for Polaris brought in their wake?

Essentially they amounted to changes in 3 vital areas. Firstly, management changes were needed. Secondly new work standards had to be implemented to meet the more precise needs of nuclear engineering, and thirdly, there would be changes in the workforce itself to provide new skills.

The management changes were widespread, and from the top of the structure downwards. A four page company newsletter in March 1966 contained a whole page of management changes from board level down to Ship and Project managers.

Robert White Johnson, whose father had served Lairds as a Director since 1920, had been the Managing Director since 1951. It was Johnson who took the yard into the nuclear building arena and it was he who suffered for the delays and difficulties that occurred when construction began.

Johnson has provided a powerful insight into some of the ills that befell the yard during the Polaris years. When asked about the effects of the cost-plus contract he has stated...

"I reckon it may have contributed to the company's failure. Once people know that they are going to be paid in any case your bargaining position is undermined, the workforce is more prone to strike and management yield to the pressure. In short, the company is open to exploitation. What is required is an understanding between management and the workforce."

In 1968 he was replaced in his position by Sir Leonard Owen. Owen was not a shipbuilder and was introduced to the workforce in a newsletter (19) as "a member of the newly formed Atomic Energy Authority, who was knighted in 1956 for his part in the successful operation of the Calder Hall reactor station." Plainly Owen was a nuclear technocrat brought in to shake things up.

During these years Cammell Laird news letters and magazines were full of details of the many changes that took place, from management moves to new job titles. These include such titles as Chief Polaris Executive, Polaris Shop Manager, Polaris Operations Manager, Polaris Personnel Manager and so on.

Viewed from a traditionalist standpoint perhaps the most important change was the introduction of quality control procedures. In some areas their introduction was gradual but in others it was very sudden. Under normal circumstances the quality of Admiralty contracts would be monitored by one or two Naval overseers who were appointed to the builders yard.

The technical specifications and standards required to build nuclear submarines needed an enormous effort on the part of Cammell Laird who had no previous experience of nuclear work.

According to the Royal Institute Of Naval Architects this was...

"an historic occasion; since for the first time in the United Kingdom a naval contract, or as far as is known any ship contract, required the shipbuilder to set up a separate organisation within the firm to be responsible for quality...to be independent of production and reporting directly to management."(20)

This quality control programme had to bring a fresh approach to a traditional industry, and be applied to the most difficult to build of all ships, a submarine. Some idea of the magnitude of the testing required can be appreciated by the fact that in each Polaris submarine there are about 30,000 brazed pipe joints (21), and that for every single one, detailed information on mill specification, chemical composition, brazer identification and date, ultrasonic examination, hydraulic pressure test and noise short positioning, had to be meticulously recorded. To cover all the testing required on a Polaris submarine approximately 1000 different test documents were needed.(22)

Quality Control in any organisation can mean different things to different people. To the client it is one method of endeavouring to secure the required standards of the quality of his purchase and so provide a greater degree of satisfaction to the end users.

To manufacturers, and shipyards manufacture ships, quality control can be a hindrance to production, slowing down the supply of materials to the production programme.

Equally contractors dislike high levels of quality control as it burdens them with responsibility to produce it and pay for its organisation. The internal conflicts produced by the divergent interests of quality control and Production have been laboured long and hard by Management Consultancy / Work Study gurus of the past like Gilbreath and Halsey. The workforce themselves, who are subject to precise quality control scrutiny, can also take typically diverse viewpoints.

Some see it as an aggravating nuisance, preventing them from building ships and doing their job the way they have always done it. Others consider that they gain kudos from being involved in a job that attracts high levels of quality control, feeling that this 'star' job provides him and his skills with status in the eyes of his fellow workers. While yet other members of the workforce may perceive quality control as a method of milking the job, enabling them to take extra time on the work, perhaps even overtime to complete a continuous process like welding, thus making the whole project last longer and hopefully keep them in gainful employment.

In the case of Cammell Laird management the negative aspects of the high levels of quality control were invalid as the Admiralty paid for the build up and running of quality control systems as a direct production charge (23).

It seems clear that Cammell Laird were convinced that Polaris was the shape of things to come and...

"that it would prepare them for the revolution, bound to take place, when nuclear power was applied to merchant ships and surface ships of the navy ."(24)

High standards of work and the systems necessary to ensure them presented Cammell Laird with three difficulties. The first was to recruit into the shipyard the necessary quality control expertise. This was not a straightforward process; even as late as March 1966, by which time both submarines were on the slipways, only some 60% of the required recruitment had been achieved.(25)

The second was the perceived need to "indoctrinate the labour force" amongst whom "quality control is not an inherent feeling."(26)

The response of the workforce to this indoctrination process will be covered in more detail later. However the third vital change apparent during the Polaris years is the change in the workforce itself.

At its peak in 1969 the yard employed 11,400 men with an average employment figure of 8,280 for the years 1960-1964.(27) The increase to cover the Polaris work amounted to almost 40%. Many of these new men were specialists, quality control men, weapons engineers, draughtsmen etc. although there was also a requirement for the more traditional shipbuilder tradesmen. Welders especially were at a premium. Vickers, as the lead yard, took advantages of a recession on the Clyde (28) to recruit suitable men. Lairds was less fortunate, facing competition for these tradesmen from the new Vauxhall Motor company factory which opened in November 1962 at Ellesmere Port.

A spokesman for the Vauxhall Motor Company confirmed this...

"We were recruiting on the mechanical side, plant fitters and particularly shipyard welders, people who had experience, coded welders on heavy welding...we were particularly interested in the type of welder that Cammell Laird trained and they did slot in very nicely...we also took electrical people, people with machine tool experience...in the mid to end sixties when jobs were readily available in the Merseyside area, I can remember we needed to recruit 2000 people within a 3 month period; it was difficult because Cammell Laird were recruiting in similar numbers."(29)

Birkenhead, not withstanding its shipbuilding roots, could not supply Lairds with the skilled personnel required, and significant numbers of targeted trades were being poached by other employers.

R.W.Johnson recalls...

"We had the other element on the Mersey too, we had the motor industry at Ford Halewood and they weren't altogether cooperative. They were pinching our men and we were pinching theirs."(30)

New men came into the yard, men that had never worked on ships, or in shipyards, much less on nuclear submarines. Men came from Crewe, Manchester and North Wales, the word was out that Lairds had a big job on, with good pay, and needed men.

Don Siddorn, a foreman millwright said...

" We lost some good men to the car industry, there were rumours of big money outside...a lot of Polaris nuclear men were not submarine men...had no submarine ideals and were simply money chasers, if another job came up anywhere else that paid better money they were off like a shot."(31)

Colin Harrison was such a new man. Manchester born he had served his apprenticeship in the locomotive industry at Gorton and Crewe. He recalls...

"There had been a big strike when I was at Air Products, I got fixed up in Lairds and travelled every day from Llangollen, most of the lads from Crewe soon followed. There were quite a lot travelling then."(32)

These seem to be totally divergent points of view. On one hand new men were seen as money chasers, on the other hand they were seen as seeking job security. These views will be further explored later on. It is sufficient for the moment to note that the former viewpoint was that of a Lairdsman aged 60 with 45 years service, whilst the latter is that of a contractor, who was no less a tradesman, but was used to travelling.

There was also a sort of middle ground involving those men who knew the shipyard and its ways but traded their skills in the market-place to achieve for themselves the best possible standard of living.

One of these was John Haggerty, a highly skilled and experienced welder. He returned to Lairds, a place which he plainly had a great deal of affection for, when he saw the chance of some job security, despite having earned more as a travelling contractor...

"Lairds is like a magnet, you always seem to go back, I always liked working in Lairds, it's crazy I know...I used to love going to work...I like welding...you really enjoy the company...at times you get fed up, soaking wet or having to brush the snow off the staging, but I enjoyed it being in Lairds."(33)

Elements of the workforce like John had an ambivalent relationship with the yard and are the most difficult to understand. But they were there and some for different reasons than others. The men who came to Lairds for the money were to prove a key factor in the behaviour of the whole workforce. There was though yet another facet of this changing workforce. The contractors, what Norman Roberts a Boiler-makers Shop Steward called BDM's or "Back Door Merchants".

Lairds could not cope with all of the work themselves. It became necessary therefore to sub-contract some work to other companies like Telemeters and Troops. Whether or not the sub-contractors were as selective as they may have wished to be in their selection and recruitment procedures is debatable.

According to one worker Colin Harrison, a coppersmith, organisations like Deeside Welding "were being offered a deal by Lairds to supply labour, working for Lairds...there were a few outfits like Telemeters doing it".(34)

One ships Manager Ronnie Owens stated..."I knew that a lot of M.I.D.(Machine Installation Dept) fitters actually left the yard and went working for subbies (sub-contractors) and came back on more money plus out of town living allowances. That causes a lot of unrest among the workforce which didn't help matters a lot."(35)

A Back Door Merchant was a worker who had obtained a union card purporting to be a bona-fide time served man. They obtained their card from a union branch office whose officials were prepared to issue it and in the process contravene union rules.

Workers, according to welder Norman Roberts "came from all over the place. One source was DYSONS in Liverpool, they used to take lads in and train them to be welders. They thought Cammell Lairds was a bloody Fort Knox.(36) (Norman was referring to the contents of Fort Knox and not the difficulty of gaining entry!)

At this point it is necessary to return briefly to to the Quality Control changes that came to Cammell Lairds with Polaris. As stated earlier Cammell Lairds had difficulty obtaining the specialist expertise required and were lagging behind Vickers in this department. Many of the new Quality Control men were new to shipbuilding and new to Cammell Lairds. They were mainly outsiders and evidence suggests that they were not welcomed with open arms into the yard, especially those whose function was to police and monitor the work. They would either get short shrift or end up getting sucked into the system of doing as little as possible for as much money as possible.

The Cammell Laird workforce during this period consisted of all of these disperate groups of men. It was a huge workforce which Lairds had not seen since the heydays of the second world war and the years immediately following.

These changes that Cammell Laird was experiencing, management changes, a new standard of work, and a changing workforce were to make the Polaris years good ones, apparently for all concerned, but they were to be the last of the good years. To provide a fuller answer to what Polaris meant to Cammell Laird and its management, it is necessary to look again at the company's attitudes against the labour backdrop described.

Did Cammell Laird pull the cloak of a very big and lucrative contract over themselves to shield them from the cut throat world wide shipbuilder competition? There is some evidence that they did.

According to the local press in 1963...

"The Polaris order came at a time when Lairds was running down on naval work," and when "the company was at its wits end to know how to find employment for the specialised teams of technicians built up over the years."(37)

If Lairds really were at their wits end then the order certainly provided the perfect tonic enabling them to undertake a major reconstruction of the Yard. In order to provide the facilities that the Polaris construction would require, in 1963/4 Lairds made considerable capital expenditures, notably the modernisation of No.1 and 2 Berths (slipways) in the South Yard, the construction of the new heavy or high welding bay and new plant, new offices, testing and inspecting facilities, stores and pipeworking shop and pickling plant. With very little other remunerative work at the yard it is interesting to ponder how Lairds managed to re-equip for the Polaris contract.

It may be that the Admiralty alone paid for these facilities, however detailed investigation is difficult as these submarines remain operational and much of this detail remains classified. Cost details are almost impossible to obtain and the only figures available in the public arena are from Janes Fighting Ships.

fig.4	SSBN Table of Costs			
MoD No	Ship Name	Builder	Commissioned	Cost in £m
01	Resolution	Vickers	Oct 1967	40.24m
02	Repulse	Vickers	Sept 1968	37.5m
03	Renown	C. Laird	Nov 1968	39.95m
04	Revenge	C. Laird	Dec 1969	38.6m

Source: *Janes Fighting Ships*, 1977 / 78.

A clue to who eventually paid for the modernisation may be gleaned from a further statement from the Chairman, R. W. Johnson, in 1963, that "the firm would be laying out capital in the region of £1M for the Polaris orders. Negotiations were underway with the Admiralty as to how much would be the naval share of the outlay."(38)

It seems that Cammell Laird was to receive an enormous financial incentive just to take the contract on, at the expense of the Treasury. This, coupled with the cost-plus attraction of the job would further ensure Lairds dependence upon government policy, and bolster the yards belief that they would always be working at the frontiers of shipbuilder technology, and would continue to be rewarded for it in the same way.

It also seemed perhaps, that the company was in a very comfortable position. Despite the regular complaints in company magazines, newsletters and annual reports about 'cut throat world competition', 'uneconomic conditions prevailing in the British shipbuilding industry' and 'depressed freight rates', there are strong indications that the company did not go out of their way during these years to pursue new merchant orders.

As early as 1964 Lairds publicly announced their reluctance to accept an invitation to tender for the new £22 M Cunarder to replace the *QUEEN MARY*. The Birkenhead News reported that..."vital stages in the construction of Polaris submarines could occur at similarly important times as in the building of a great liner...in these circumstances it could be that they (Cammell Laird) might feel that they should voluntarily decide not to tender for the Cunard vessel."(39) - and ultimately Lairds declined the invitation to bid for the new 'Queen'.

Ships manager Ronnie Owens, a mechanical engineer, has clear memories of preparing a tender for the Q4 as it was then known,

"In the early 60's I was working in the drawing office on the Q4 tender on the piping system...I remember that the first set of tenders were scrapped because Cunard hadn't accepted any of them. I don't know if Lairds ever went in for it again."(40)

It appears that Lairds were interested in this big merchant contract in 1960/62, but the client decision to freeze the work in order to re-evaluate the market or the ships specification, had the effect of putting the job out to re-tender some 18 months to 2 years later.

By this time Polaris contracts had been signed and work had started. In the words of the managing director;

"we had a contract to build and we were on our way. Yes, at that time we would probably be fighting shy of merchant work."(41)

Polaris seemed to have a strangle hold on Lairds and in November 1966 the Lairds Director and Polaris Project Manager S. Fawcett announced that;

"for the next year the company has a smaller merchant ship programme to allow for an all out effort on Polaris."(42)

Just how much smaller is shown by the number of keels laid in the next year and the very limited amount of fitting out work. These tables illustrate the dependency of Lairds on Polaris and the strength of the Admiralty hand in pushing the progress of the job.

The smaller merchant programme forecasted by Fawcett, provided just 9 months of fitting out work, the bulk of work on any ship, and then on just two small car ferries.

fig.5	**Keels laid 12 months following November 1966**					
Ship No	Name	Type & Tonnage	Keel Laid	Launch	Handover	
1330	Conqueror	Hunter/Killer Nuclear Sub	5.12.67	28.8.69	9.11.72	
1331	Könign Juliana	Car Ferry	18.5.67	2.2.68	7.10.68	

fig.6	Vessels launched post-Nov 1966 to Dec 1967*			
Ship No	Name	Type & Tonnage	Launch Handover	Work provided post-launch
1323	Ulster Queen	Car Ferry 4478	1.12.66 31.5.67	5 months
1324	Nuclear facility Barges for MoD (N)			
& 1325	(approx 25 ft x 25 ft pontoons with small workshops on top)			
1326	Lion	Car Ferry 3333	8.8.67 21.12.67	4.5 months
1327	Number not used			
1328	Herland*	Bare Hull (Shelter Dock DVC) 497*	13.12.66 13.12.66	Nil
1329	Norseman	Bare Hull Bulk Carrier 29259*	20.5.67 27.5.67	1 week

* Source Cammell Laird contract records pages 101-102. 1328 Name and Tonnage and 1329 Tonnage

not available in Cammell Laird records - details obtained from Lloyds Register of Shipping 1971 - 72.

Cammell Laird did not have the experience that Vickers, the lead yard had, and the tight building schedule for Polaris ran parallel with Lairds learning cycle. They had to learn to build and build to learn at one and the same time, a daunting prospect for any shipyard. Their performance was invariably between 10 and 13 months behind that of Barrow, despite the fact that Barrow was racked with stoppages due to industrial disputes in the later 60's, whilst Lairds, as mentioned previously, had just one, and that, comparatively short lived at the very onset of the work.

	Principal stoppages at Barrow and Birkenhead for the 5 years ending			
fig.7	December 1968 (5,000 or more working days lost)			
Area	Date of stoppage	No of workers involved	No of working days lost	Cause or object
Birkenhead	16 Mar 1964- 5 June 1964	1,260	54,000	Claim by shipwrights for a wage increase of 1s per hour.
Barrow	13 July 1964- 20 Oct 1964	135	7,900	In support of a claim for an increase in wages.
Barrow	5 June 1968- 3 Dec 1968	420	39,800	Protest by apprentices against the introduction of a new pay structure.
Barrow	1 July 1968- 12 July 1968	920	72,000	In support of a claim for parity in repair allowances.
Barrow	3 July 1968 still in progress Dec 1968	1,845	166,000	Inter-union demarcation dispute over allocation of certain work.
Barrow	9 Sept 1968 still in progress Dec 1968	70	5,400	In support of fitters and apprentices already in dispute.(see above)

Source: House of Commons Debates, Vol. 778, Cols 323-324, 26 February 1969.

The learning cycle was more than just absorbing the new Nuclear technology. Lairds were dealing with experienced and worldly wise builders of nuclear submarines. Vickers at Barrow held the whip hand and took every opportunity to improve their own position, often at the expense of Lairds. A Polaris Ships Manager, Ronnie Owens, is convinced that this was the case...

"Vickers ordered all the equipment and it all went to Barrow, from there it was directed down here to Birkenhead. Frequently material for the second boat would go to the third one, so that 03 (*REPULSE*) was further ahead than 02 (*RENOWN*), which was our first boat. I feel that they (Vickers) were trying to prove that they were the cream of nuclear shipbuilders."(43)

For Lairds 1967 was a year spent bring 02 (*RENOWN*) to the fitting out stage and getting 04 (*REVENGE*) off the slipway. Both vessels were to be moved into two dry docks ringed with security fences, that were to be their home for the next 22 months.

The reasoning behind awarding Cammell Laird the contract for Ship No.1330, *HMS CONQUEROR*, a nuclear, non-Polaris attack submarine, in August 1966, is worthy of scrutiny. One school of thought was that the yard was already late with the Polaris boats; though the quality of work was apparently high. In addition the taxpayer had already paid for the modernisation of the yard so why not capitalise upon it?

It seems more likely however that Lairds were given ship no. 1330 to provide a reservoir for the skilled labour which, due to the variability of the Polaris work, could simply be 'standing by'- on pay and non-productive. Once more Lairds management appeared to have interpreted this as a positive sign of their arrival in the big time as a nuclear shipbuilder, despite the efforts of Mr. Roy Mason, the Minister of Defence for equipment, in January 1967, to increase the building pace within the yard.(44)

Lairds management now began to give the impression of seriously getting to grips with their problems, realising perhaps, that the 'Gravy Boats' would not last forever. They might also have believed that some strong words would bring them into favour in the Ministers eyes.

An extract from a Cammell Laird newsletter in September 1967 provides an illustration of this new harder line - A message from M. J. Wyatt, Director, to the workforce...

"There is clear evidence that some workers are not pulling their weight...the men who waste time in berth side and dockside accommodation...who read papers during working hours, have unofficial tea parties and who find any excuse for not working...defraud the company, defraud their colleagues...and defraud themselves of higher wages."

The letter continues;

"men will be checked regularly to see whether they are on their jobs, and men consistently missing will be dealt with firmly but fairly....if the improvements which are vital to the companys' prosperity do not come about...we will have to consider a more serious approach."

On this note the newsletter ends. Could there be a more serious approach? The message was strongly worded. Did the company really mean business or was the tough talking after the award of the *CONQUEROR* contract instigated by Lairds political masters, as a veiled warning that times were not as good as they had been.

If the management were now attempting to address the yards problems maturely by taking such a line, did it work?

The men seemed to believe that the thinly veiled written threat would not be actioned. The view of nuclear welder Norman Roberts is typical

"It was only being said on paper..not doing it physically"(45)

The workforce seemed to know as much as anyone else, that the good times would not last forever.

The picture is one of a large workforce, both on the management and labour fronts, fighting to realise tough timescales but fundamentally flawed and, seemingly, unable to solve their more basic problems.

The first experimental submarine built at Lairds in 1915, the *E41*.

The first ever all welded sea going vessel in the world, the *FULLEGAR*, built in 1920.

HMS RODNEY, completed in 1927.

She is flying the White Ensign and therefore was probably leaving to or returning from Acceptance Trials.

The largest floating dock in the world in 1912.
Built at Birkenhead it is pictured here on test in Portsmouth lifting the 'Super Dreadnought' *HMS MONARCH.*

The cruiser *HMS ACHILLES*, completed in 1933.

The Battleship Prince of Wales at sea. On this ship Winston Churchill and President Roosevelt signed the Atlantic Charter. She was sunk by a Japanese torpedo in 1941.

The first purpose built Aircraft Carrier, *ARK ROYAL* in Cammell Lairds wet basin circa 1938.

A very rare photograph of the launching of the submarine *THETIS* in 1938. She was tragically lost on sea trials off Anglesey in 1939 taking 99 men with her. The loss of the *THETIS* is the worst submarine disaster in British history. The submarine adjacent to the empty slipway is the *TRIDENT*.

The launch, in 1934, of the 1000th ship built at Cammell Lairds. The 5000 ton cargo liner *CLEMENT* for the Booth Steamship Company of Liverpool.

The passenger liner *MAURETANIA* slides into the River Mersey in 1939.
Spectators can be seen all the way along the river front.

The second aircraft carrier built at Lairds to be named *ARK ROYAL* seen at a Naval Review. She was completed in 1955.

The launch of the *WINDSOR CASTLE* by the Queen Mother in 1959.

A magnificent example of Cammell Lairds craft. The passenger cargo liner *RMS WINDSOR CASTLE* launched by the Queen Mother in 1959.

Britains first gas turbine powered guided missile destroyer *HMS DEVONSHIRE* launched by Princess Alexandra in 1960. Seen here just after launching being guided into the wet basin.

This unusual photograph shows two famous Birkenhead built vessels in service. The *ARK ROYAL* with the *DEVONSHIRE* in the foreground.

Preparing, in 1963, for the Polaris Project that was to dominate the yard for the next ten years. The construction of a new "high welding bay" can be seen and an old tracked steam crane in the foreground.

No.3 16th Oct 1963

What the Polaris contract meant to the workforce.

What were the attitudes of these men towards the acquisition of additional skills required for nuclear work or the increased levels of surveillance necessitated by the new Quality Control procedures? How did they view the job financially? Did they understand what cost-plus contracts meant to them and their shipyard? Did any moral doubts about nuclear weapons exist? How did the actions of the workforce reflect their thoughts and ideas?

I have already referred to the mix of people that made up this significantly increased workforce, the outsiders, the sub-contractors, the B.D.M's, the men who were established employees and those shipyard men who had gone elsewhere and returned to Lairds.

Other than the fact that they had a common employer this diverse workforce had a fragmented identity.

Within it there were three fundamental attitudes or concerns. In no particular order, they were...

A)   The money they could earn and what that could do for them and their families.

B)   The ease with which they could get money for doing as little as reasonably possible.

C)   The sometimes vague and at other times strong sense of pride in being a shipbuilder associated with the Polaris project.

As far as the latter point is concerned the work is still vividly remembered by many of those involved but, having been completed there is a sense of loss which perhaps can be explained by the role of the Polaris boats and the fact that, unlike other warships, they are rarely in the news.

Most people in the town of Birkenhead have a strong association with the shipyard, even if only to attend a launch as schoolchildren. There are few people in the town who could not identify famous names like *MAURETANIA* and *ARK ROYAL* as being Laird built ships. Yet many have stated that they had no idea that half of Britain's nuclear deterrent was built in their local shipyard.

This is a puzzling phenomenon. Perhaps the Polaris years were a chapter in the yards history that is best forgotten, after all, many of these men, their brothers of their fathers or their friends, witnessed the end of the Polaris contract, the dire straits that the company of Cammell Laird was left in, and the mass redundancies that were the result.

In an effort to understand the workforce a great deal of reliance has been placed upon the views expressed by many of the workforce that have been interviewed. Opinions, clearly based on hindsight, have been separated from the attitudes that prevailed at the time. The final distillation is believed to be more accurate in sum than the individual attitudes encountered.

Polaris was undoubtedly well paid in comparison with other manufacturing industries of the period yet the documentary evidence to support this is at best sparse. Despite assistance provided by Cammell Laird, wage records for 1960-1970 do not appear to exist. Other than interviews evidence of levels of pay to the workforce has been dependent on limited documentation from some Trades Unions and that of the more rare shipyard worker who has kept old pay slips for 20 years! Nonetheless the evidence of those interviewed clearly indicates that pay was high.

Jimmy McGrath, a stager recalls...

"Oh aye, the gravy boats...men would be working on a job and think, by Christ it's hot in here; we shouldn't be working in these conditions. So they would see their shop stewards, who would see the management and that's how a lot of these allowances came about. Once a man saw his docket at the end of the week, and the allowances showed a certain number of pounds, it was a sharp intake of breath. It was a known fact that everybody on Polaris made good money. People used to say how many houses you bought or have you got a new car. There is no doubt about it Polaris was the plum job in Lairds for the money."(46)

Charlie Kelly, a shipwright, remembers the period:

"Polaris gave us three nights overtime as well as Saturdays and Sundays plus allowances. You could treble your basic earnings...people all of a sudden bought motor cars...had bank books etc...me and my missus were very cautious, we lived in a corporation house, we couldn't appreciate that I would be working the following week...

"............When I worked on the shiprepair side I was used to getting 'finished up every 3 or 4 weeks. It took me many years to realise that I had security of a sort. Suddenly I had a bank book and I could plan ahead, then we looked at ourselves and decided that we could by a house...I had saved a few bob, that I hadn't been able to do before."(47)

One shipyard workers wife who was present contributed to the interview...

"we did have better standards than other people around us that weren't in Lairds. We ran a car, we dressed our daughter very well, we had a stereo. I remember the other wives at the shops — they would say to me...it's alright for you, we all know where your husbands working." (48)

It would be straightforward to provide many more extracts of interviews in the same vein. Jimmy McGrath, the stager, talked about allowances being an important part of the pay. Allowances were additional monies paid over and above the hourly rates for enduring the special kinds of conditions that occur during the construction of submarines, such as heat, dust and very confined spaces.

Allowances were not new and were derived, even in the Polaris years, from an original allowance agreement between the shipbuilders and the Trade Unions established in 1915. On the construction contract for the Polaris boats every single worker who set foot on the submarines or on part of the submarine at the pre-fabrication stage was paid a 'condition' or 'body allowance' of 4d (1.6p) for every hour on the job.(49)

Thus a man in receipt of condition allowance and with some 60 hours on his clock card, (which was not excessive on Polaris), could expect an extra £1 in pay. This was at a time when a tradesmans weekly pay for a normal week with no overtime was around £17.

The limited information available on pay relates to the middle 60's. Pay rates for Engineering Trades in the Shipbuilding and Ship repair industry were obtained from a survey of rates supplied by shop stewards of the district office of the Amalgamated Engineering Union in 1965. The table below shows the parts of this document relevant to Cammell Lairds.

A Comparison Weekly Wage Rates for Local Companies in 1965*

fig.8

	Fitter	Turner	Semi-skilled
Cammell Laird	334s	360s	295s
Crichton Brown	304s 11½d	-	-
William Cubbin	305s	305s	-
Mersey Docks & Harbour Board	305s	305s	253s 4d
J.E. Hall	334s 8d	-	-
J.A. Mulhearn	304s 11½d	323s 8½d	-
Lever Bros**	305s 6d	305s 6d	-

* Weekly pay rates - Shipbuilding and Shiprepairing Industry. Rates calculated by District Office from Shop Stewards Quarterly Reports - 1965. Issued by Amalgamated Engineering Union Liverpool District Office 31.03.66
** Source: Lever Bros Ltd.

These rates of pay refer to all engineering trades in all the Merseyside shipbuilding and shiprepairing yards. Looking first at Fitters rates an examination reveals that although Cammell Laird differentiate between toolroom fitters, plant fitters and outside fitters, their average rate in this survey is 334 shillings (£16.70) per week. With the exception of one very small company, who were refrigeration specialists, this was the highest rate on Merseyside by almost 20 shillings (£1.00) per week, or on these sort of pay levels 6%.

Next, Turners. Lairds had 3 classifications, Heavy Lathes, Medium Lathes and Machinists. The average rate for these trades in 1965 was even higher at 360 shillings (£18.00). This was by far the highest rate in the area, some 36 shillings (£1.80) or 11% more than their nearest rivals.

Even without a bonus Lairds semi-skilled men too earned over 40 shillings more than their counterparts in other industrial sectors.

In comparison with other industries outside the shipbuilding arena, Lairds personnel were much better off. For example, Lever Brothers Ltd., the soap manufacturing giants based at Port Sunlight, paid their fitters on average 28 shillings (£1.40) less per week.

The engineering trades in Lairds at this time did significantly better than they would have working for other local companies, in or out of the shipbuilding industry. What is vitally important to this analysis is that none of the Lairds rates quoted includes submarine allowances.

It is hard to pinpoint the progress of these allowances due to so few wage records at the shipyard but some documentation is available. A memo from W. H. Owens (Ships Manager for Ship No.1330 *HMS CONQUEROR*), to Mr. Gartland (Time and Wages Office) refers to "Polaris body allowance agreement of 22 July 1966 and 17 February 1967, by which the body allowance was increased to 1 shilling (5p) per hour."(50)

Another agreement between the company and the Confederated Shop Stewards Committee dated 8 September 1967 increased the body allowance for Polaris to 1 shilling and eightpence (8.3p) per hour. (51)

These allowances were paid for every single hour, to every man on Polaris work, regardless of trade or skill, or whether working normal hours or overtime.

Such payments, to tradesmen, semi-skilled men and even un-skilled men and apprentices, were, according to a memo dated 20 June 1965, signed by the Time Office Manager Mr. Algeo "conceded...contrary to general practice."(52)

Polaris was not only breaking new ground in technical terms it was setting new payment precedents. A Millwright foreman stated that...

"People were getting rises every 3 months. Some people were getting more in allowances than they were actually getting in wages."(53)

Coded welders, who had to endure the highest temperatures whilst working to exceptionally high tolerances, could earn allowances that were more than double the body allowances in 1965. Given the rate of body allowance increase already seen, and that the Polaris contract was not completed until the end of the decade, it is reasonable to conclude that the allowances for these welders increased as well.

When welding special Polaris steel, known as QT35, welders could receive an hourly allowance of 2s 6d (12p). This was in addition to an hourly rate of between 7s 6d (37p) and 8s 6d (42p), effectively a 35-45% uplift in hourly rate.(54)

Jimmy McGrath perhaps encapsulates the sort of money that was being earned in Lairds during the Polaris years,

"There were that many different allowances, dirt, heat, fibreglass, you name it...thats all people used to talk about you see...it was a topic of conversation all the time...many men turned down a foremans job because foremen were not paid overtime or allowances."(55)

Despite the dearth of records, clearly the workforce in Lairds were doing very nicely out of the Polaris contract, yet the sub-contractors did even better. They would receive the same money as Lairdsmen plus travelling money and in some cases lodging allowance.

A Ships Manager stated...

"I know a lot of the fitters actually left Lairds and went for more money with sub contractors...on more money plus out of town allowances."(56)

The wages received by Lairds workforce during this time were "very, very high" due to the large amounts of overtime which was needed and the many allowances available. The question must be asked whether Lairds obtained value for money? Did the workforce earn the pay levels they received?

A quarter of a century on the value of the Lairdsmens work is proven by the end results. *RENOWN* and *REVENGE* form one half of Britain's nuclear deterrent and fulfil this task thoroughly and satisfactorily.

The true cost of these vessels cannot be cannot be known with any certainty, due to the very nature of the product. The only comparison possible is to try to identify the value of the work done during construction against the wages paid for that work.

Shipyard workers, according to view put forward "don't rush out to work unless they have to...they only come to work for the money, the maximum amount possible for the minimum amount of work."(57)

By comparison management see things differently, and require,

"The maximum amount of work for the minimum amount of money."(58)

These opposing viewpoints obviously indicate the potential for conflict between management and workforce. To further complicate matters, these contrary views come from one and the same man, a former tradesman in Lairds who later became a member of the management team.

Lairds were behind schedule and yet suffered no major industrial disputes during the period. They had lead yard experience from Vickers, the only British yard with any previous nuclear experience. Yet Vickers themselves were racked with strikes.

This begs the questions, how could this be? Were the men working hard enough for their money? Were the management managing? Was there overmanning and waste?

Polaris, as a simple structure, could not physically accommodate the number of men that were booked to the job:

According to one Ships Manager...

" On 1316 (*RENOWN*) in AMS 1 (Auxiliary Machine Space) and AMS 2 we had six fitters on days in each compartment and six fitters on nights between the two. When it came to the second boat 1317 (*REVENGE*) the Manager in AMS 2 had 28 fitters on days alone; thats 28 fitters plus all the other trades...given the compactness of that compartment, I don't know how they got in...basically there were 28 names booked to the job, but I don't believe that there were 28 people working there...there was a lot of fiddling going on...people coming in and going straight over the wall."(64)

Being over the wall in shipyards is nothing new but on Polaris it had become an art form. One man stated that...

" I used to do 7 twelve hour nights...but I would only be there for say fifty of those hours at best...we used to give the timekeepers 2s 6d (12p) and they would clock your card for you...they must have been the best paid men in the yard....we used to go into the time office some nights and they'd all have the desks pushed back to the wall and be playing 5 a side football."(60)

Where was the supervision and management? Who was checking the work done and who was doing it? Lairds were using advanced planning techniques like CPA (Critical Path Analysis) and had, as well as Admiralty Overseers, a large and expanding Quality Control Department. All these people were supposed to be doing the watching and the checking on top of the normal supervision provided by the chargehand ,foreman, manager system.

One worker is quite sure that there was some agreement between the watchers and the watched:-

"It was soft overtime and a lot of men, especially the blue-eyes*, could get away and get paid for it, they weren't there, they were all over the wall...if your face fitted you could do handstands, if your face didn't fit, well you had to stay on the job. Even if you weren't working, you had to stay there."(61)

Such a lax situation could only have happened with a workforce that was almost out of control and a management that was cushioned from the harsh reality of profits and losses more usual in the building of merchant ships.

Not only did the cost plus contract encourage such actions it provided the yards management with an excuse for industrial peace at any price. There are no shortage of pointers to the view that Lairds adopted a softly-softly approach towards the trade unions. As a direct result of this the unions had great difficulties in accepting the hard realities that came at the end of the Polaris contract, when the yard was in trouble and full scale redundancies were the order of the day.

This conciliatory stance towards the unions weakened the position of first line management like foreman and chargehands, some of whom genuinely tried to organise things better. However when they saw that more senior managers gave in so easily, they too tended to adopt a less responsible attitude.

One Polaris manager remembers..

"We had to meet the director every week and he had meetings by ships compartment, say Monday-Torpedo, Tuesday-Control Room, Wednesday-Reactor etc...I had 3 areas on the boat so went to 3 morning meetings each week. Things would come up that required answers... but he wouldn't wait until the next meeting...he'd want them right away...so you'd get the answers and ring up his secretary and say you'd got the information, when can I see him? I would have to make an

* shipyard slang for a favoured or favourite worker.

appointment...but the A.U.E.W. convenor simply knocked on the door and walked straight in."(62)

Ironically, from the mens point of view it seems that the last thing they wanted was an industrial dispute. The money was good, the overtime plentiful, and the allowances excellent. No major stoppages for the whole programme indicates a contented workforce. A shop steward who considered that he had a strong case for a walk-out recalls calling a meeting:

"You couldn't use Polaris as a weapon...that 75% of the workforce were happy with their lot and soft overtime, more soft than hard...the glut of the men were on Polaris you see...but they didn't want to know...imagine yourself at a mass meeting calling for action...75% of the men on Polaris and 25% on merchant work, which way will the vote go? It will go with Polaris obviously."(63)

Yet Lairds management must surely have been aware of such meetings and must have been conscious of the high levels of pay that Polaris men were receiving. So why did they consistently bow to union pressure?

Certainly the cost-plus nature of the contract did not encourage conflict but a further clue may be provided from other evidence from a foreman:

"It was a well known fact that Lairds needed naval work to build merchant ships. A lot of the costs of Polaris helped to build some of the merchant vessels that in the yard at the time. If the boss had used up all his hours on a boat he'd have to start Booking to Polaris...working on a merchant ship, like a car ferry, and booking the men to Polaris..all the foremen did it, including me."(64)

This view is supported more guardedly by a Ships Manager,

"I didn't have any assistance from 'common' work...but I heard of instances...like when we were preparing the tender for the St. Edmund, a car ferry. It was the labourers hours, the engine labourers. I remember saying that we cannot build it for that, those man hours, and someone said Oh! but the actual engine labourers hours for the *KONIGIN JULIANA* (a car ferry built during the Polaris years) which was the same size, are within that figure...I said I'm sorry but its got to be twice as much. Later I made some inquiries and found that during overtime much of the machinery in the 'Juliana' had been shipped by labourers who were supposed to be working on Polaris."(65)

Clearly some of the Polaris overmanning was not overmanning in the true sense of the word for all of the time. The use of labour costed to Polaris, effectively subsidised some merchant building, providing yet another economic cushion from competitive commercial risk and thereby negating any requirement for a disciplined financial approach.

Such practices indicate that the contract was truly one that allowed everyone involved in it, from labourers to the board, to enjoy high remuneration for a very long time with little or no incentive to attempt to increase productivity or effectiveness.

The management and the workforce knew full well that at the end of the day they would be paid and paid well. It didn't matter if the job had to be done 2, 3 or 4 times. If a part was wrong it was wrong and if a new one was needed the money would be forthcoming.

One worker speaking about waste said:...

"They might make three pipes, none of which would fit, so they would just chuck it in the dock, or cut up the cupra-nickel and take it home to weigh it in. "(Weighing in means literally to take materials like copper or brass or Cupra-Nickel, out of the shipyard and to a local scrap merchant would pay cash by the weight of the material)

"A job could be done 2 or 3 times and nothing whatsoever was said about it...

"....One shop steward who was there ran a pipe straight through a ladder, so that when you went down the ladder you ended up with a bloody pipe between your legs! There was so much waste. If you put in a pipe from A to B, anything which came along later would have to be re-routed. Nothing was very well planned as regards what was fitted in first. You never knew what a pump was going to look like. You could see a bed but not the configuration of the pump, and you never knew when it would be arriving. Nobody would ever come up and say...don't run that pipe there or it will foul the pump if you do. Nobody."(66)

The conclusion drawn is that the men worked at their own pace, in their own time, with their own quality levels and that they booked many more hours than they were actually present for. The supervisors, very few of whom had nuclear experience, or even any submarine experience, were so busy running around for materials, Quality Control inspectors and drawings, that they had little time to actually coordinate the work of the men, who were in such large numbers as to make them very difficult to police. Some supervisors too were sucked into the 'Gravy Boat' syndrome, allowing men to disappear or do no work and this would make the job last longer; an all win situation albeit in the short term. At all levels the management seemed to have resigned themselves to living with the situation.

Slow progress was being made with the build of both submarines, and the bills were being paid regularly.

What is more difficult to assess, is how much of this conciliatory doctrine was an unspoken directive from the government or the Admiralty, who may have been aiding and abetting the situation. After all, the taxpayer would foot the bill and accountability was almost impossible for a project that was for Britain, to provide an effective deterrent.

These vessels were a first for the nation and for Cammell Laird and it is quite revealing that despite the big money and the fiddles that went on, the men who built Polaris refuse to criticise the end result, including the standard that these ships were built to.

The respondents interviewed for this book revealed a harrowing tale of waste and indiscipline. How is it possible then for sometimes extreme displays of pride to be evident? Pride is a difficult concept to explain, and when this explanation is coupled with the same men that threw materials into the dock it becomes even more complex. There is a paradox in attitudes, on one hand these men were quite open about the fact that they were using subtafuge and were slacking on the job, and on the other hand, have, as craftsmen, a strong sense of pride in their work.

For example, in response to a question about the possibility of deliberately lowering standards on the job, to make it last longer, one man replied...

"No, we were working in submarines for the Ministry. We're not talking about some bloody box that allows a man to jump ashore. The Quality Control was tremendous...we never lowered our standards. If a submarine goes wrong then men die."(67)

Are these people the same ones that had been described by the Naval Overseer at Birkenhead, M.P.C .Oliver, as having 'no inherent feelings for Quality Control?' Shipbuilding and the pride of shipbuilders is nothing new, some men shed tears at the launch of a vessel, or at the loss of another. Shipbuilders see themselves as providers of instruments that rule the waves. The pride and satisfaction were most certainly there with the Polaris boats...

"Its a nice feeling though, to complete a nice looking job, especially if its a big complicated job."(68)

Those respondents interviewed in their own homes, or at their work, without exception, had some shipbuilding relic either hanging on the wall or close at hand, from a large oil canvas of the aircraft carrier *ARK ROYAL* that dominated a living room, to an ash tray 'liberated' from the *OCEAN MONARCH*.

Whilst the pride was very evident in a completed job, some were dismissive of some completed work.

" I never went to launches myself, to me it was an everyday thing...like a baby being born isn't it? I never cheered at a ship going down. To me it's just a job I've been involved in and it's finished."(69) or, "lots of it was tongue in cheek...the Chairman would say 'and three cheers' and the lads would cheer...more or less taking the mickey out of the Chairman and the launch party.(70)

The truth is complex and hard to focus upon. There appeared to be genuine warmth from many men toward the Polaris contract; it was a technically complex job and the ultimate conquest of these complexities is worthy of pride.

But pride is tinged by a gulf between the workforce and the company, as if the ship, its construction and completion are events that could not have happened without the craft and skill of the workforce, and the absence of management would have made little or no difference. The feeling is summed up by an anonymous shipyard poet!...

"If managers were blades of grass
And foremen grains of sand
One half of Lairds would be a field
The other desert land."

Perhaps the thing that taints the pride of building the Polaris boats comes from the knowledge that these vessels were the last big job that Lairds had before the financial crash of 1970. This was the end of the gravy train and it was a tragedy of epic proportion. People may or may not wish to remember Polaris, but they do remember the end of the job, and the fact that it coincided with the economic collapse of the local shipyard allows a natural link to be made, and maybe perceive Polaris, with hindsight, as the ruination of Cammell Laird and Company, Shipbuilders and Engineers.

So was Polaris the beginning of the end for Cammell Laird? Even the most cursory look at the companys profit and loss accounts, would see how dramatically the Polaris contract restored the fortunes of the company from the relative doldrums of the late 1950's and early 1960's

The Cammell Laird +Co. annual report for 1968 stated that;

"Cammell Laird and Co. (S+E) made the largest single contribution to our profits...a feat which deserves hearty congratulations."(71)

Yet just one year later net losses on shipbuilding were £2.5 Million, resulting in the government acquiring 50% of the equity of the company and the amputation of the now impoverished shipbuilding arm of the Cammell Laird Group from the more prosperous parts of the organisation.

What happened in just one year to push a thriving business into the depths of bankruptcy? Simply that the goose that laid the golden eggs had moved on. The future nuclear submarine building programme of Britain was to be continued at Vickers yard in Barrow. Lairds were out in the cold.

Early in 1969 the Ministry of Defence announced that all future business for the construction of nuclear submarines would be placed without competitive tender at Barrow.(72)

R. W. Johnson recalls...

"The time has come very suddenly, when the bottom dropped out of everything, and one was left looking around and saying where's my next order coming from. You've got all these men in the yard, what on earth am I going to do. We were very disappointed. When we took Polaris we were given to understand that there would be follow-on nuclear orders...it was a risk that the management took and we were prepared to take it, because we thought there would be a follow-on." (73)

It is impossible to be privy to verbal contracts or half promises that may or may not have occurred during the negotiation of the contract, and it is probably fair to say that Lairds had little or no alternative than to accept the contract with open arms as both national and international competition for orders was very strong. However, the evidence from the Chairman and Managing Director of the company resists any challenge. Lairds were promised that there would be more to come, and believed that once the Polaris work was complete they would be in a position to offer unique expertise worldwide and capitalise upon it, as shown by the managements earlier optimism about nuclear propulsion for all types of vessels. It did not happen and both the company and the men felt let down.

Opinions vary between those who were casualties of the redundancy programme that was inevitable in light of these events, and those who, by good luck or good judgement, were kept on at Lairds until they retired or are still working at Lairds today. Typical of the formers opinions about the importance of the Polaris contract was that of a nuclear welder:...

"It ruined it...they saw it as a good job there, they thought they had landed in Utopia...but bad management spoiled the yard...we had a lot of outsiders coming in chasing the money...there were so many dead heads...and the management was weak, they were out of touch, if Polaris had never come to Lairds, Lairds would have been a better place." (74)

Or the latter type of workman, still working in Lairds, asked if Polaris helped his career at all,

"I'd like to say no, but in fact we were complemented on our work by the head foreman, who'd had it from the directors...I'd like to say no because I think Polaris on the whole didn't do the yard any good."(75)

Management and workforce should accept equal responsibility for burying their heads in the sand throughout the 1960's Polaris building project. Political pressures apart, Lairds failure to expose themselves to the competition from Japanese, German, and in the 1960's, Italian shipbuilders, can only be laid at the door of management.

The profits were undoubtedly available from Polaris work to establish a leaner, fitter shipyard that could have succeeded just as easily as it has failed. Polaris was a golden opportunity that slipped through the company's fingers.

The end of the line for the yard was summed up by one man who was both a reactionary and a romantic.

"I would have liked to have found somebody who would listen, and say to them, new machinery is needed here, to help us build bigger and better ships; we cannot do it on our own. All we could hear were government people who were high-ups, saying that the working man was lazy...we were hard working...but we couldn't work harder because we hadn't got the equipment to work with."(76)

Modernisation did come to Lairds in the end.

In 1972 the Government announced its intention to finance the upgrading of the yards facilities culminating in the erection of a covered construction hall 147 metres long, 107 metres wide and 50 metres high. This facility was not completed until 1978, one year after the company had been nationalised as part of British Shipbuilders. Also in 1972 the old camel symbol of Lairds was finally retired and replaced by the designer logo monogram shown below.

In the same year there was another memorable milestone. For the first time in the yards history, the honour of formally launching a vessel was given to an employee. The bulk carrier *OAKWORTH* was launched by Mrs. Ellen Smith, an office cleaning supervisor and the companys longest serving female employee.

The yard worked on, with a much reduced workforce, and still relied heavily on warship building with the contract for three type 42 guided missile destroyers, *COVENTRY*, *BIRMINGHAM* and *LIVERPOOL* providing the backbone of the order book. A car ferry, the *ST. EDMUND*, small motor vessels and petroleum product carriers made up the rest.

Another first for Lairds was delivered in 1983. The Oil Platform *SOVEREIGN EXPLORER* which was built using dry docks 6 and 7 instead of the traditional slipway method of construction. The platform itself straddled the two docks and was supported by four huge legs, two in each dock, which were in turn supported by a huge pontoon in each dock.

This work too was hoped to be the first of many, but as with so many other Laird firsts, it became the only one ever. The company was quietly getting on with business, hoping for better times ahead. However in comparison with the rest of the worlds shipbuilders these orders seemed no more than scraps from the table, too small to be bothered with.

The "bigger and better ships" that the Lairdsman knew he could build were being built elsewhere.

Modernisation came too late, yet not too late for Vickers, who were also quietly getting on with business, the big business of continuing to build the next generation of nuclear submarines.

The denationalisation of Cammell Lairds coincided with the award, to Vickers, of the contract to build all four of the next generation of nuclear submarines, armed with Trident nuclear missiles.

The Birkenhead yard became a subsidiary of the Barrow yard in 1985.

The rest, as they say, is history.

The new "high welding bay" is now complete (April 1964) and the new jetties are taking shape. The ship under construction in the foreground is, I think, the *SAMARIA* a cargo liner for Cunard.

Launch of Polaris submarine *HMS RENOWN*
Cammell Laird ship no. 1316, in February 1964.

Launch of Polaris submarine *HMS REVENGE*
Cammell Laird ship no. 1317, in March 1968.

HMS REVENGE being towed from the Mersey to the safety of Lairds Basin after her launching.

The official handover of *HMS REVENGE* in December 1969, effectively the end of the 'Gravy boats'. The dockside accommodation that men would have to be chased out of (myself included) can be seen on the right of the picture, while on the left is an unarmed polaris missile.

77

The Gravy boats sail away from the Mersey and take with them any future Cammell Laird may have had.

A rare photograph of *HMS CONQUEROR*, the Birkenhead built Hunter Killer submarine, ship no. 1330, which caused consternation upon her return to Britain, after sinking the Argentine heavy cruiser *GENERAL BELGRANO* during the Falklands conflict, by flying the Jolly Roger.

The end of the road. Upholder class submarine *HMS UNSEEN* rolled out ready for lanching in 1990. Together with her Lairds built sisters URSULA and UNICORN these were the last ships of any kind to be built at Cammell Lairds.

The Nuclear Question

Before concluding this look at the Polaris years in the Birkenhead shipyard of Cammell Laird and company, some mention should be made of an ancillary sphere of interest, the nuclear question.

To exclude any comments on the morality of building nuclear weapons in a book about the building of Britain's still active and only Nuclear deterrent would leave the book incomplete. No position of judgement is taken by the writer on this issue which, by itself would probably serve as the subject of another whole book and would probably provoke a good deal of argument and counter argument.

The building of warships has been the backbone of the company since the very beginning and so nothing is new in a sense except that at the time of building these vessels were the very pinnacle of modern naval weaponry, in much the same way as the *ALABAMA* before them.

Shipbuilders are the heart of the matter and it is the effects or otherwise, upon their hearts and minds whilst constructing such powerful weapons that is interesting. When Mrs. Edna Healey, wife of the then Minister for Defence, Denis, launched ship No.1316 H.M. Submarine *RENOWN* on 25th February 1967, her words at a post launch lunch were:

"If I could add anything to the traditional words for the launching ceremony, they would have been that as we saw this deadly ship going down to the sea, in our hearts we hope that she will never be called upon to use her terrible weapons."(77)

The men who built Polaris were asked...

"Did you have any feelings or ideas about what you were building?"

The overwhelming response was one of part divorcing the ship from what she does, and part divorcing the ship from the domestic situation.

The material prosperity that the high levels of earnings on this job provided for many men and that Polaris was the springboard for some of them to aspire to owner occupation, motor cars and bank accounts, has, I hope, already been illustrated.

Often Polaris is remembered for adding a worthwhile contribution to a career, or a curriculum vitae;

"Any new work that came along I adapted myself to it: I was being watched and people noticed, I made a name for myself on Polaris submarines...and that resulted in my promotion."(78)

Or another view

"It helps on the C.V., I have had experience of nuclear work. I've had other jobs on Inspection and it all stems from doing that work at Lairds...two years after leaving Lairds I was made foreman, and have never been back on the tools since."(79)

To deny men the capacity for thought is to consider them empty vessels, yet most respondents "never really thought about it at the time.", but with hindsight and the provocation of the question itself, would do the same job again;

"You looked at it just like doing a job, and everybody had them (Polaris), I think...and if your working it doesn't matter what you're working on if it's paying your bread and butter and your mortgage and that...it doesn't matter does it...in one way...and anyway, you tend to think that these things won't be used."(80)

Most of the workforce on these submarines vividly recall the protest marches by the Campaign for Nuclear Disarmament and some of the walls in the neighbourhood around the yard still bear the graffiti of the protesters. 'PEOPLE NOT POLARIS'. However the shipyard men pushed this aside as they would a wayward lump of steel on a berth, they simply stepped over it.

Their concerns were with earning a living for them and their families the only way they knew, by building ships. A ship that carries nuclear weapons is the same as a ship that carries bananas. It's work.

On a positive note it is quite clear that some men gained from having this nuclear experience, with it's high standards of work and its in depth Quality Control procedures. Those who found work elsewhere or stayed in Lairds don't consider that it did them any harm at all, in fact, quite the opposite, in some cases it enhanced their market opportunities.

Conclusion

When Cammell Laird had been officially announced, in May 1963, as the shipyard that would build one half of the Polaris fleet, it was hailed as

'preparing Lairds for the revolution, bound to take place, when nuclear power was applied to merchant ships and surface ships of the Navy.'(81)

Patently this revolution did not happen. Nuclear propulsion was to prove expensive and this is one reason that Lairds failed to carve for itself a nuclear future. If Britain was to maintain a nuclear force it would be small, and the thinking of progressive governments has channelled this business to just one shipyard with no room for Cammell Laird.

The wisdom of this decision is questionable from a number of different viewpoints. If Lairds was 'the only serious contender' (82), other than Vickers, to build nuclear submarines in the 1960's, what precluded Lairds from being a contender in the future? Certainly Lairds built Polaris submarines took longer to build than those in Vickers, but the physical shipbuilding process compares well up to launch time, only an average of 1 months behind Vickers. It was in the fitting out stages that they fell behind. How much of this was due to the lead yard ensuring its own position in the driving seat by controlling all incoming materials and information? Some of the evidence suggests that this was so. Therefore Lairds track record may not be as bad as the figures suggest.

Because of the classified nature of these vessels the only available costs are those shown earlier, and by comparing the cost of each pair of vessels from this limited information, the Lairds built ships cost just over 1% more than the Vickers built submarines.

Considering that Vickers had nuclear experience and Lairds had none, then it is reasonable to say that the costs at the Birkenhead yard bear favourable comparison with Barrow. Also, in light of the differences in industrial relations problems between the yards, the decision to give all future nuclear submarine work to Barrow seems inexplicable, yet today, Vickers in Barrow are building Trident submarines.

It is true that Cammell Laird are involved in the Trident project, but not as an independent company, only as a subsidiary of Vickers; Lairds involvement in nuclear work today was obtained at great cost to the company: government bale-outs, massive redundancies, nationalisation and de-nationalisation have stripped the shipyard down to a shadow of what it once was.

But a revolution did take place in the 1960's. The explosion in the size of oil tankers and bulk carriers, as shipowners began to see the benefit of economies of scale after the 1956 closure of the Suez canal. It is well known how Japans yards took advantage of the situation, building technically simple ships, essentially large floating boxes with an engine at one end. Could Cammell Laird have got into the act had Polaris not arrived? Perhaps they could have.

By 1962 a new 950 feet long x 140 feet wide dry dock had been completed, and extensions to slipways No. 4 and No. 5 by 900 feet and 850 feet respectively.(83)

These facilities were specifically designed to provide for the building of 'super tankers' up to 100,000 tons, well in excess of any British built tanker at the time. In fact Britain did not produce its first 100,000 ton plus tanker until 1965.(84)

Maybe Lairds could have been in on the ground floor of the super tanker boom, as the Japanese, good and cost-effective as they were, did not have, in the early 60's, limitless capacity. Whether Lairds could have maintained momentum as the Japanese surely did, can only be speculation, however the fact remains that the chance was there.

The evidence clearly indicates that the workforce was too big. The push to build Polaris was of such proportions that...

'Cost, although a sensible and important matter, was not as salient a factor of the programme as time'.(85)

Overmanning was on a grand scale as were the fiddles that were happening all around, from men over the wall and claiming overtime hours, allowances etc., to the "assistance" given to the relatively small throughput of merchant work, that of costing some its labour to the Polaris contract.

Many workers prospered from Polaris, as did the shipyard itself at the time, but the lessons are all too easy to see. Cost-Plus contracts kill. They are dangerous and open ended and ask very little in return. Can the workforce be blamed for taking advantage when they see so many of what they perceive to be hangers-on arriving at the yard, and management changes so regular, that it seemed like musical chairs? Can the workforce be blamed for not appreciating what life would be like after Polaris, by which time the Japanese had all but cornered the market? A fact which seemed to have taken the world by surprise, much less the workforce in one British shipyard.

Or can the management be criticised for the same error of judgement? Arguably it was their job to be aware of world trends, and the reconstruction programme of the early 1960's indicates that they were, until the Gravy Boats arrived when they seemed to shut their eyes to that which was going on around them.

Cost plus contracts of this nature originate with governments and policies. The shipyard of Cammell Laird was faced with a "build it now and build it quick" philosophy, with economic considerations as a secondary aspect. This is a fatal error as has been proven in Cammell Lairds case. Management are absolved from any commercial accountability and companies grow fat and slow on easy profits. Any thoughts of negotiations with labour that may be contrary to the progress of the contract and its steady profit contribution, are avoided. If a metaphor can be forgiven, nobody wants to rock the boat.

The author knows that some readers may see parts of this book as somehow doing the shipyard of Cammell Lairds and its workforce a disservice, a blot on a famous history. This has not been the intention. Far from it. The shipyard of Cammell Lairds was the provider for many families including mine.

It gave me and many others the chance to acquire a skill during our formative years, skills which were used by me as the most solid and dependable foundation to a career. In later life a university education became possible, yet I am as proud of my indentures as my degree certificate.

The yards great history speaks for itself and perhaps, as mentioned earlier, just needed to be recorded again in a new way.

This work about the Polaris contract is simply an attempt to explain why the shipyard failed, and failed at such a crucial time. For once Lairds were not in front. Shipbuilding technology had changed at a furious pace while they were building Polaris submarines. Blame is for others.

Meantime the men at Lairds today continue to use their skills building submarines. For how long nobody knows.

Perhaps this book might help understand why many of them look back on the "Gravy Boats" as the beginning of the end for a place that they and I hold in great esteem.

POSTSCRIPT
Margaret want's rid of shipbuilding.

1993 saw what was once known as Cammell Lairds handover yet another submarine to the Royal Navy. *HMS UNICORN* the last of four Upholder class vessel, conventionally powered but exceptionally quiet running, vital in todays navy, in which stealth is perceived as of greater importance than firepower.

But things change - the final irony for Cammell Lairds was revealed only weeks before *UNICORN*'s departure. The Upholder class submarines were declared surplus to requirements in the latest Defence Review. They are to be sold off to the highest bidder. These four brand spanking new submarines cost the British Taxpayer £900 million!

The firepower for the British navy of tomorrow is to be provided by four of the next generation of nuclear powered and nuclear armed submarines. Trident.

These four vessels, the cost of which is almost impossible to estimate, are under construction at VSEL shipyard at Barrow, Cammell Lairds lead yard of the sixties. In the heady denationalisation days when Lairds was swallowed up by it's "Big Brother" the talk was of work-sharing, "a sensible decision given Lairds nuclear experience", the "trickle down effect to Lairds of such a big contract".

It would be unfair to say that Lairds had not had any of these promises kept. Some sections of Trident have been fabricated at the Birkenhead yard. These have, however been only a cosmetic sharing of the work.

The reality of "Lairds" is somewhat different. Lairds is on the rocks again.

The parent company wants all the work for itself.

Lairds was the subject of political jockeying for position and rhetoric. A "save our shipyard" campaign was launched by the local press and pressure groups. A desperate search to find a buyer to take control of the yard failed.

However...thanks to the success of this book you are now reading a re-printed version, and, as with all such things, hindsight and information not previously available make judgements easier.

Recent statements by Sir Robert Atkinson, former chairman of British Shipbuilders 1980 - 1984 are now on public record stating that the when he presented his case to the government, in 1981, for the future of British Shipbuilding, he was told by an as yet unnamed very Senior permanent government officer,

"Robert, Margaret wants rid of shipbuilding. Remember that."

The 'death warrant' for Cammell Laird was signed as early as 1985, in that most hallowed of all European political institutions, E.C. Headquarters in Brussels, and neither the Cammell Laird management or workforce knew anything about it. The Conservative government of the day led by Margaret Thatcher, accepted £140m in European aid and in return killed off nine British Shipbuilding yards, one of which was Cammell Laird in Birkenhead. Her chief hatchet man in this sacrificial demise, was, according to the same source, Mr. Norman Lamont, he of "we have no intention of leaving the E.R.M." fame. As my dad would have said, "and the band played 'believe it if you like'."

When Cammell Laird was designated, by the E.C., as a warship building yard in 1985, it was automatically denied access to the Ship-building Intervention Fund (S.I.F), a mechanism by which the ship-building industries of E.C. nations that were engaged upon the building of merchant ships could obtain subsidies upon their pricing policies.

The so called "hidden agenda" of the time was the fact that their was no going back should the situation change, which, once again with hindsight for us mere mortals, it did; with the advent of the collapse of the Soviet Union and the resultant "peace dividend."

In 1985 Norman Lamont said of the S.I.F. in a written answer to the House of Commons on July 5th....

'Aid of this kind will...not normally be appropriate for, nor provided to, yards which have been or are to be privatised by British Shipbuilders.'

Sir Leon Britain, one time Conservative Chancellor, now spending more time with his family, is now on record as stating that...

'If Cammell Lairds warship designation were to be changed...the European Commission might ask for some of the aid back.' (Perish the thought). He also stated that...

'In 1985 the British Government undertook not to grant Intervention Fund Aid to Cammell Laird in future as part of an overall reduction in capacity...which was required as a counterpart to authorisation of a package of aid to British Shipbuilders.'

Cammell Lairds shipyard in Birkenhead has now closed. Mothballed for a while, but the 'smart money' is on redevelopment as a leisure centre / theme park / marina / light industrial units of the kind that we are all too familiar with. Incredible as it may seem investment grants will almost certainly be available to assist with any redevelopments.

Cammell Laird had proven, over nearly two centuries, that they were more than capable of building the biggest and the best merchant ships, be they passenger liners or oil tankers.

Why then were they denied the chance to fight it out in the world market using the same S.I.F. that other "Community" nations had access to?

Famous naval and merchant vessels that defended this country, the men that manned, and often died, on them apart;

The pioneering engineering spirit of this shipyards history apart;

The strikes and chequered industrial relations history of all shipbuilding yards in Britain apart;

The building of one half of Britains then "necessary" nuclear deterrent apart;

The thousands of men who lost their jobs at Cammell Laird apart;

And perhaps saddest of all, those countless young people for whom the Cammell Lairds of this country will never again provide any real life training or skills apart.

The answer is as simple as it is, in my view, disgraceful.

Margaret wanted rid of shipbuilding.

Bibliography

1.   Cammell Laird company magazine No.4 August 1964.
2.   Cammell Laird company newsletter No.5 February 1967.
3.   Cammell Laird company newsletter No.5 February 1967.
4.   Evidence from interview Norman Roberts.
5.   Evidence from interview Fred Tooley.
6.   Builders of Great Ships. Published by Richard Garrett Services Sevenoaks, Kent 1959.
7.   Cammell Laird and Co. Contract records Pages 96-99.
8.   Cammell Laird and Co. Annual Report and Accounts 1959 and 1960.
9.   Cammell Laird and Co. Annual Report and Accounts 1963.
10.   Cammell Laird and Co. Annual Report and Accounts 1964.
11.   Cammell Laird and Co. Annual Report and Accounts 1965.
12.   Birkenhead News Editorial March 11th 1964.
13.   Birkenhead News Editorial March 11th 1964.
14.   G. M. Dillon. 'Dependence and Deterrence, Success and Civility in the Anglo American Nuclear Relationship.' Gower 1969. (Hereafter: Dillon- Dependence and Deterrence.)
15.   John Simpson. 'Lessons of the British Polaris Project; an Organisational History.' Journal of the Royal United Services Institute. Vol.70 March 1969.
16.   Cammell Laird and Co. Annual Report and Accounts 1964.
17.   Dillon-Dependence and Deterrence.
18   Evidence from interview Don Siddorn.
19   Cammell Laird Newsletter No.11 1968.
20.   H. J. Tabb and S. A. T. Warren. 'Quality Control applied to Nuclear Submarine Construction.' Quarterly Transactions, Royal Institute of Naval Architects 1966 Vol.108. (Hereafter - Tabb & Warren- "Quality Control".)
21.   E. H. Hunter. 'Quality Control for a Polaris Submarine.' Welding and Metal Fabrication. November 1967 Vol.35.
22.   Tabb and Warren. 'Quality Control."
23.   Dillon - Dependence and Deterrence.

24. Birkenhead News. May 1963. Statement by R. W. Johnson.
25. Tabb and Warren. Comments of Naval Overseer at Birkenhead Mr. M. P. C. Oliver.
26. Tabb and Warren. Comments of Naval Overseer at Birkenhead Mr. M. P. C. Oliver.
27. Cammell Laird and Co. Annual Report and Accounts 1960/1964, 1969.
28. Dillon - Dependence and Deterrence.
29. Evidence from interview. Personnel Spokesman for Vauxhall Motor Co. Ellesmere Port.
30. Evidence from interview R. W. Johnson. Chairman and Managing Director of Cammell Lairds 1951-1968.
31. Evidence from interview Don Siddorn.
32 Evidence from interview Colin Harrison.
33 Evidence from interview John Haggerty.
34 Evidence from interview Colin Harrison.
35 Evidence from interview Ronnie Owens.
36 Evidence from interview Norman Roberts.
37 Birkenhead News May 25th 1963.
38 Birkenhead News May 11th 1963.
39 Birkenhead News January 18th 1964.
40 Evidence from interview Ronnie Owens.
41 Evidence from interview R. W. Johnson.
42 Cammell Laird newsletter No.3 1966.
43 Evidence from interview Ronnie Owens.
44 See for example The Times 31st January 1966.
45 Evidence from interview Norman Roberts.
46 Evidence from interview Jimmy McGrath.
47 Evidence from interview Charlie Kelly.
48 Evidence from interview Mrs. Barbara Tooley, wife of Fred.
49 Letter from Cammell Laird Personnel Dept. to Amalgamated Union of Engineering Workers 21.3.60.
50 Letter from W. H. Owens to Holmes/Gartland, copies to M. J. Wyatt 28.3.69.

51   Agreement between Cammell Laird and the Confederated Shop Stewards Committee 8.9.67. Signed for the company by M. J. Wyatt and for the committee by P. J. Riley and H. Murt.

52   Memo from Cammell Laird personnel dept. to M. Algeo, Time Office Manager. 20.6.65.

53   Evidence from interview Don Siddorn

54   Letter from Cammell Laird to Mr. F. Derrig, Amalgamated Society of Boilermakers, Blacksmiths and Structural Workers, confirming Polaris agreement. 23 June 1965.

55   Evidence from interview Jimmy Mc Grath.

56   Evidence from interview Ronnie Owens.

57   Evidence from interview Charlie Kelly.

58   Evidence from interview Charlie Kelly.

59   Evidence from interview Ronnie Owens.

60   Evidence from interview Colin Harrison.

61   Evidence from interview Norman Roberts.

62   Evidence from interview Ronnie Owens.

63   Evidence from interview Norman Roberts.

64   Evidence from interview Jimmy Mc Grath.

65   Evidence from interview Ronnie Owens.

66   Evidence from interview Colin Harrison.

67   Evidence from interview Charlie Kelly.

68   Evidence from interview John Haggerty.

69   Evidence from interview Norman Roberts.

70   Evidence from interview John Haggerty.

71   Cammell Laird and Co. Annual Report and Accounts 1968.

72   Cammell Laird and Co. Annual Report and Accounts 1968.

73   Evidence from interview R. W. Johnson.

74   Evidence from interview Fred Tooley.

75   Evidence from interview Don Siddorn.

76   Evidence from interview Fred Tooley.

77   Cammell Laird newsletter No.5 February 1967.

78   Evidence from interview Jimmy Mc Grath.

79   Evidence from interview Colin Harrison.

80   Evidence from interview Colin Harrison.

81   Birkenhead News 25.5.63.

82   Dillon - Dependence and Deterrence.

83   Cammell Laird Reconstruction Works...May 1960. Wightman Mountain Ltd. Westminster.

84   Ewan Corlett. 'The Revolution in Merchant Shipping' H.M.S.O. "The Ship"...1981.

85   Dillon - Dependence and Deterrence.

Brief Outlines of Respondents

1   **Fred Tooley**   Coded welder and foreman for a short time on Polaris. Aged 57, married with one married daughter. Works as a welder today, but not at Cammell Lairds.

2   **Norman Roberts**   A Boilermaker's shop steward during the Polaris years and a member of the Communist Party. Aged 55, a single parent. Unemployed for twelve years.

3   **Don Siddorn**   A millwright at Lairds since the age of 15. Aged 60.

4   **Robert White Johnson**   Former Chairman and Managing Director of Cammell Lairds and Co. (S&E). Now retired. Aged 79, married with three children.

5   **Colin Harrison**   A coppersmith. Manchester born and apprenticed in the locomotive industry. Worked on Polaris as a direct employee and as a subcontractor. Aged 44, married with three children. Still in the trade, but not at Cammell Lairds.

6   **Ronnie Owens**   A mechanical engineer. Aged 46 with two children. Still works at Cammell Lairds.

7   **John Haggerty**   A coded welder. Apprenticed in the Jarrow shipyards and a third generation shipyard welder. Aged 66, retired. A widower with two children.

8   **Spokesman for the Vauxhall Motor Company Ellesmere Port**   Involved in the build-up of the car manufacturing plant throughout the 1960's. Has always worked in the personnel department. Now a personnel manager.

9   **Jimmy McGrath**   A stager, ultimately a foreman stager. Aged 62 and retired. Married with one child.

10   **Charlie Kelly**   A shipwright, time-served at Lairds. Worked on Polaris throughout the period. Aged 57, married with two children.